Seven Sins

for a Life
Worth Living

Also by Roger Housden

How Rembrandt Reveals Your Beautiful, Imperfect Self:
Life Lessons from the Master

Ten Poems to Last a Lifetime

Ten Poems to Set You Free

Risking Everything: 110 Poems of Love and
Revelation (EDITOR)

Ten Poems to Open Your Heart

Chasing Rumi: A Fable About Finding the Heart's
True Desire

Ten Poems to Change Your Life

Sacred America: The Emerging Spirit of the People

Sacred Journeys in a Modern World

Roger Housden

Seven Sins

for a Life
Worth Living

Harmony Books
New York

Published in the United States by Harmony Books, an imprint of the
Crown Publishing Group, a division of Random House, Inc., New York.
www.crownpublishing.com

Harmony Books is a registered trademark and the Harmony Books
colophon is a trademark of Random House, Inc.

Library of Congress Cataloging-in-Publication Data
Housden, Roger.
    Seven sins for a life worth living / Roger Housden.—1st ed.
    Includes bibliographical references.
    1. Pleasure.   2. Life.   3. Conduct of life.   I. Title.
    BJ1481.H68 2005
    171'.4—dc22   2005016591

ISBN 13: 978-0-307-33671-2
ISBN 10: 0-307-33671-9

Printed in the United States of America

DESIGN BY ELINA D. NUDELMAN

10 9 8 7 6 5 4 3 2 1

First Edition

For Maria Housden,
who, more than anyone, has helped me
appreciate much of what I try
to communicate in this book

contents

9

CONTENTS

Did you take pleasure in it?

THE TRADITIONAL LITMUS TEST FOR A SIN
ACCORDING TO THE CATHOLIC CHURCH

Seven Sins

for a Life
Worth Living

When you die,
God and the angels
will hold you accountable
for all the pleasures
you were allowed in life
that you denied yourself.

ANONYMOUS

introduction

I met a woman in Georgia once, she was a Playboy bunny, all long legs and heavy mascara. In the town she grew up in, she said, in Tennessee, dancing was against the law. You might have thought America would have learned back in the twenties, in the days of the speakeasy, that prohibition only encourages what it seeks to quell.

Pleasure, especially in countries of a distinctly Puritan persuasion like ours, has had a bad rap for a very long time. Life, so the conventional wisdom goes, is too serious to be taken lightly.

The birth of this country did not arrive on wings of joy. The first generation of settlers included long-faced men in tall black hats who took their life and religion seriously. They didn't have time for smiles of pleasure or sighs of delight. They were too busy working. They were utilitarians; if it's not useful, why do it or think it? Good Puritans that they were, work, like cleanliness, was right up there next to godliness. America was built on hard work, and the tradition continues today.

Nothing wrong with that, of course. All this work has got America where it is, and there is no doubt that without the work ethic and the drive to succeed, nothing much of anything would ever have been achieved, discovered, invented, or sold. No books would have been written or masterpieces painted; there would be no Empire State Building or Trump Tower.

Americans are famous for both working and playing hard. We are the most competitive, driven nation on earth. We win far more Olympic gold medals than most other countries put together. Our unique brand of football resembles a modern gladiator contest. Our military devours more dollars than all other aspects of national life combined. The education system itself is a battlefield. Parents jostle to place their infants in the best strategic positions as soon as they are born. Life coaches, fitness trainers, therapists, diet coaches, golf coaches, preschool coaches, even coaches to help you die well—there are professionals to cheer you through every stage and aspect of life.

The more hours you spend in the office, the more multitasking you can do, the fewer vacations you take, the more your professional and also your social credibility increase in stock. You are a good, productive, and useful person if your diary is crammed for the foreseeable future, and even more so if your e-mail in-box edges past the one-hundred-a-day mark. Your stock soars higher still if you happen to mention that you thrive on four or five hours of sleep a night. Eight hours a night is for losers who have nothing to get out of bed for in the morning.

No wonder America is number one. The desire to achieve the great goal of being a winner begins in the cradle and only stops when you drop. It has produced a nation of incredible achievers. No one else has put someone on the moon. Few others have run faster or played harder. No one else came up with a Google or can equal a Microsoft. No other street in the world has the power of Wall Street. American initiative, enterprise, ingenuity, and sheer persistence are second to none. And when you are not working your career, why, that's no reason to be idle—you can work on yourself! You can get a fitter, trimmer body, a more balanced mind, a cleaner spirit. Not only psychological but also spiritual success is just the next frontier when the world's achievements seem to pall.

Seven Sins for a Life Worth Living goes the other way, against the cultural grain. It claims that a driven life is not much fun, and if there's no pleasure in it, then it's hardly worth living. It encourages you to be pleasure-prone. It is a cry for freedom: freedom from the breathless and guilt-laden need to be constantly productive and useful. It is all for a warm, juicy, and satisfying life that is not beholden to righteous beliefs of any persuasion.

Taking pleasure is an *attitude* more than an activity. These pages celebrate sensual pleasures but also the pleasures of being foolish, of doing nothing useful, of not being perfect, of not knowing, and more.

Pleasure is the food of the soul as well as the senses, sustenance for the spirit as well as the body, since pleasure can lead to delight, which can easily lead to joy, and joy is the upwelling of the human spirit, which always lives and breathes beyond the confines of right and wrong. "Energy is eternal delight"—the poet William Blake was thinking of just such a joyful upwelling when he wrote that line.

Some pleasures, of course, are culturally encouraged, such as the pleasure of good company and fine wine, or the pleasure of a good book. But there are many more that, for reasons of social or religious probity, have long been deemed unworthy of a responsible member of society. This book specifically aims to revalue and celebrate these guilty pleasures.

Chocolate cake happens to be a favorite of mine, but that's not the kind of guilty pleasure I have in mind. The deepest forms of pleasure are those that fill us with a sense of meaning and joy. You will find here attitudes and ways of being in life that can foster a sense of delight and ease; that can allow us to live life in a more spontaneous and joyful manner. Which does not mean, however, that pleasure always comes easy.

Researchers have distinguished three levels of happiness: what they call the pleasant life, the good life, and the meaningful life. The pleasant is the one based on the experience of instinctual pleasures—raw feelings and sensation thrills. The second is what Jefferson had in mind, speaking of the pursuit of happiness. He was picking up on Aristotle's idea of being able to exercise your talents in a favorable environment. Third, the deepest and most pleasurable aspect of fulfillment, or happiness, is a sense of meaning, which always consists in attaching to something larger than ourselves.

Conventional wisdom, however, tells us that nobody goes to heaven for having a good time. We genuinely think pain is virtuous, which is not surprising given that the majority of us worship a crucified Savior. Suffering is a great purifier, a forger of character, no doubt about that, but why make a career out of it when it comes unbidden anyway? True pleasure is a far rarer and thus, one would think, a more precious gift.

The last time you were full of joy (when was that?) you didn't think to debate with yourself whether you were doing the right thing or not. Joy is full-bodied, wholehearted, all-encompassing. In a moment of joy you are no longer a kingdom divided—between right and wrong, this way or that way, should or shouldn't. The divisions, if they do come, come only later, when the moment has passed.

With all its abundance of achievement, just where is America today? It is the economic engine of the world. It is the consumption giant of the world. But do we take pleasure in all this consumption? Is it giving us what we need? Are we really enjoying ourselves yet? America is by far the greatest consumer per capita in the world of anti-depressants, cocaine, and heroin. A quarter-million therapists are kept busy all over the country. Not everyone, it seems, is happy. And I don't just mean those who have to live on the streets. Think of all those comfortable lives of quiet desperation, where the only consolation is a new car or a new fur coat.

In Brazil or in India you will see people who have nothing yet are brimming with life. They smile a lot, they laugh out loud. They jump and skip. In France, in Spain, in Italy, people have different priorities. They don't want to be number one. They are not as productive as Americans; their economies are good enough but not booming. Yet they seem to know what the good life is. They eat the best food on the planet, drink the best wine, take the longest vacations, surround themselves with spectacular architecture, and come up with some of the best art, dance, and music. In short, they enjoy themselves. No wonder they have fewer heart attacks over there, even though they consume more fat and a lot more wine.

And they talk to each other. On the street, in the subway car. When someone enters a restaurant in Italy, they are likely to greet the whole room. The Mediterranean is still, as yet, a civilized world. What do they know that we don't?

They know that the body and the life of the senses are good. That real pleasure, genuine enjoyment, usually takes time, especially when it's a matter of lunch. That not everything has to be useful to be of value; that a beautiful sunset serves no purpose at all. That sleep is a good thing, even in the afternoons; that laughter is another good thing, even in public. That singing (which is against the law in public places in Dallas) can lift other people's spirits as well as your own. That the human soul, by its very nature, stirs with passions that are moist and deep enough to give birth to flamenco and Beethoven. And that you don't always have to treat yourself as a project in need of improvement; that maybe, just maybe, you are fine as you are.

And yes, they acknowledge more easily than we do that it's all going to end anyway sooner or later. America is the most death-denying and youth-fetishizing culture the world has ever seen. Our collective behavior suggests a generalized guilt in response to the natural delights and pleasures of this world. (We stay too busy to give them the time of day.) Conspicuous consumption, far from being a sign of our love for life, is as much as anything a defense mechanism, a ploy to give us some feeling of permanence in a world that, and we know it, is blazing each second in its own death throe.

And so we hold on tightly, anxiously, not lightly. As if we intuit somehow that the secret of life is passing us by even as we live it; that we may well end up at the end feeling as though we were mere strangers on this earth, invisible, whatever our successes and achievements. Ultimately, it is impossible to store up riches here, and we know it. It is impossible to do the right thing all the time, to be careful, always to have your ducks in a row, and still be happy.

> *Those who are willing to be vulnerable move among mysteries,*

said the poet Theodore Roethke.[1] To be vulnerable to the mystery of our life as it presents itself requires forgoing our hopes and fears for the future and being willing to taste what is here before us, in all its poignant bittersweetness. For the only richness that leaves a trace, the only happiness worth living for, is the full-bodied sensuous and sensual experience that is possible now, right now. When we can let down the barricades and allow that we are not built to last, this moment will shine as sweetly as the moon, and we shall feast on our life.

Is this to advise a return to the sixties all over again? Could it be nothing more than an endorsement for some ecstatic Manhattan dance scene, all that orgiastic frenzy submerging the individual in a collective trance of music and drugs? That would be one way to go, and no question about it, there's a time and a place in anyone's life for zoning out. But that isn't the message in this book. Because the kind of pleasure I'm talking about here is a full body and mind thing, something you have to be around to experience if you are going to fully appreciate it. Excess only takes off the edge.

Epicurus, in the fourth century B.C., was the original advocate of a pleasurable lifestyle, and though his name has been misappropriated ever since—there are several luxurious restaurants called The Epicurean—he himself preferred moderation when it came to the appetites. He drank water rather than wine and was happy with a dinner of bread and olives. His priorities for a rich and contented life were friendship, freedom, the pleasures of an examined life, and enough food and shelter to keep body and soul together.

I would agree with the old Greek that you can't be off

in a stupor, drunken, drugged, overfed, or otherwise, and still thrill to the sensation of all your cells dancing. Neither does an armchair, or a plate of ravioli, have to be over-stuffed for you to feel you have got your money's worth. The more present and awake you are to your experience, the more likely the experience will be one of genuine pleasure.

No, the message in this book is that if you can be present to it, life is already enhanced enough as it is. And that means life in all its forms, the dark as much as the light. What the culture looks upon as bad form, and the church as sinful, is likely to be as sure a way to joy as anything. The devil is not, in any event, to be avoided, since he shares a room with your guardian angel.

There is an odd piece of sculpture at the back of Notre Dame Cathedral in Paris. A leering devil is leaning over and embracing an angel, who in turn is holding the devil. A warriorlike figure stands over and behind them, looking down at both with a compassionate eye. That warrior is our own eye of discrimination, the quiet clarity in us that is able to embrace the opposites and acknowledge the place of them both in our lives. That, rather than any outer code of belief or set of moral judgments, rather than any black and white version of right and wrong, is the quality that can offer the surest guide for how we might live. We have only to give ourselves the time to hear it.

So the purpose of this book is to inspire you to lighten up and fall in love with the world and all that is in it—and especially to lighten up on yourself. Because if you are like most people, you have already given yourself a hard enough time to last a lifetime. Lighten up—not in a blind way that refuses to see the shadows that anyone could see if they looked at your life, but in a way that is merciful; a kinder, gentler way that will allow you to flourish more in your own light and warmth.

But first let us begin at the beginning, back there in the Garden of Eden, and explore, not where it all went wrong, but what in fact was so right, so gloriously right about Eve and that scrumptious apple. And why, above all else, we are so fortunate to have the pleasure of sitting here in a human body with all five senses up and running.

To err is human—but it feels divine!

MAE WEST

Security is mostly a superstition.

It does not exist in nature. . . .

Life is either a daring adventure

or nothing.[1]

HELEN KELLER

original pleasure

It's all her fault, if you believe the old story. If only Eve hadn't bitten that apple, we would still be drinking in the pleasures of Paradise now. We would have no pain, no death, no worries. The living would be wonderfully easy. But she had to go and spoil it for all of us in a single thoughtless moment.

The old story of Eve has caused endless confusion and ambivalence about the value of being in a body and enjoying the life of the senses. It has given women a bad name. It has perpetuated a legacy of guilt and sin. Our own good sense would surely appreciate a different version. We have only to tell it another way to see that, in fact, Eve did the most brave and beautiful thing.

It must have taken a great deal of courage to reach out her arm despite all those somber warnings from the Father God. It must have taken a lot of self-confidence to make up her own mind instead of blindly obeying old Gray Beard's injunction. Eve is the perfect role model for the independent woman. She gave us the power to make up our own mind and to have a will of our own—the original pleasure that, as we know, always comes with an edge.

She went ahead, picked the apple from the tree, and bit into its ripe and ready flesh. She knew immediately that it was good, so she passed the apple on to Adam, that he might taste the goodness of it also. Oh god, that was such a juicy apple! There has never been an apple quite like that one before or since.

In that moment their eyes were opened. Adam and Eve awoke from the primordial dream. They saw the beauty of their form, and they knew—they could smell it, they could feel it—the world and everything in it was good. From that moment on they knew they were going to have an incredible ride; that life was richer by far than they could ever have imagined. Oh yes, and it was sharper, too—it hurt sometimes. But that didn't make them feel less alive, because in the very moment of biting the apple, they came to know that everything, including they themselves, was already passing away. They knew that this fleeting moment, the one that they could taste and touch and see and hear now, however beautiful or painful, would soon be gone forever. So what, other than guilt and fear, was there to lose in tasting that Golden Delicious?

Others have cast the snake as the devil, but I don't think that's the real story, either. What nobody tells us is that the snake kept close to the ground and knew the ways of the inner worlds that run deep in the earth and that ensure that the plants and all the trees grow according to their season. He was brimming with life, that old snake, and when he whispered sweet words into Eve's ear, she knew to take his wise counsel. She chose the way of knowledge when she took that forbidden fruit. Her eyes were opened to what it meant to be human, and she was more than ready to leave the safe haven of angels and take on the deep pleasures and also the risks that come with having a soft and fragile form that doesn't last long.

In the moment she took the fruit, Eve blessed all generations to come. She showed us we could wake up and have a part in creating our own world. When the snake slipped his word into Eve's ear, he fertilized her sleeping soul. She could see that life was not only beautiful but short. Better to get on with it then, she thought, and so through the pearly gates she went with Adam, and out into the light and dark of this world, leaving the eternal one behind her.

To live a sensuous life is to follow the example of Eve. You take risks. You are willing to take the pain along with the joy. You're not fooled by the old story, which would have you believe that the beauty and pleasures of this world are temptations; that they will seduce your spirit away from its true home, which is in some heaven you can fully appreciate only when you are dead.

Religions of every stripe infer that we do not belong here; that is why they urge us not to be swayed by the delights of the flesh and to keep our mind on the hereafter. Yet, not only is this a good place to be, despite all the troubles that come with the assignment, but deep pleasures come with having a body that angels will never know.

I believe in the flesh and the appetites.
Seeing, hearing, and feeling are miracles,
and each part and tag of me is a miracle.[2]

WALT WHITMAN

I say: "What are you doing at this moment, Zorba?" "I'm sleeping." "Well, sleep well." "What are you doing at this moment, Zorba?" "I'm working." "Well, work well." "What are you doing at this moment, Zorba?" "I'm kissing a woman." "Well, kiss her well, Zorba! And forget all the rest while you're doing it; there's nothing else on earth, only you and her! Get on with it!"[1]

NIKOS KAZANTZAKIS

ONE

The Pleasure

of All

Five Senses

We can see farther today than any of our forefathers could dream of seeing. We can see farther than the keenest cheetah or lynx. We can look over the horizon, around the world, up into space, down into our intestines digesting dinner. Nothing can escape our eye. We can watch practically anything we want—the only thing is, most of what we look at comes down a cable. Using the naked eye is fast going out of style. Why bother when a camera will do it better? The image is becoming more real to us than the real thing.

There is a man in England who does his bird watching in front of the television. He doesn't need binoculars. He will watch the golf tournaments for the chance flight of a heron across the green. He will watch nature programs, not for the lion strutting in the foreground, but for the little bird in the background that the commentator neglects even to mention. His greatest thrill is to identify a bird on his screen and check it off his list as "seen."

Not just our eyes, but all of our senses are losing the original savor of first-hand experience. We live in an ocean of smell but smother it in detergents, disinfectants, and artificial perfumes. Millions wear little white earphones and hear only faintly the sounds of the living world they are passing through. We are becoming out of touch with the earth we live on, and fast. We need to come to our senses before we lose them.

This physical life is to die for. When we stop for a moment to register how alive everything is—every cell of our own body, every turning leaf, every drop of rain—we can begin to catch on to the fact that all of Nature is sensual by nature.

One way this came home to me was, of all things,

from the lick of a Jersey cow. She had idled over to me at the gate of a field on the edge of the Cotswolds in England. Her slab of a tongue, hot with a steamy, grassy breath, curled out and began rasping across the back of my hand on the gate. That slow, grating rub, like a worn kitchen scourer, heaved itself lazily over my flesh with an undeniable empathy of beast to man. Less sloppy than a dog, slower of pace, more casual altogether than any animal I can think of, that Jersey cow had the time of day for me, or for anyone who cared to lean over the gate and offer their salt; for it was that she was after, however much my sentiments might have liked it to be otherwise.

It may sound strange, but that lick from a Jersey cow was erotic. The word has come to have an almost exclusively sexual connotation, but being moved and touched is always at the heart of what it means to be erotic: to be in a living, felt relationship with life, with all our senses and intelligence. In the Greek myth, where Psyche is another name for the human soul, Pleasure was the child of Psyche and Eros. Pleasure, then, is the result of the passage of Eros. It is an erotic response to life, one that is physically moving. The body shudders, quivers, and trembles with pleasure in striking some chord with the world around it.

That's one of the many good things about having a body—you can be moved and touched by, literally be in touch with, other bodies. We all love to touch and be touched, not least because it brings us to earth, to our own ground, and to the common ground we share with others. Touch is the primary human experience. It is the first sense to develop; babies can die if they are not held, and their cries are often for touch as much as for food. My wife's most cherished memory is of holding her newborn child and smelling the top of its head.

As children we are always in touch, having our hands in everything. We squeeze mud between our fingers, play with sand, pick up worms; even as adults we find it hard to keep our hands off "safer" objects like the goods in a furniture store or bread at the baker's.

Hands have a life of their own. They have a way of taking hold of things before our social conditioning has time to stop them. They finger the fresh fruit in the grocery store, half consciously brush the arm of the person we are talking to, run along the backs of wooden chairs.

My own love the firm shake of another's hand, the grasp of a doorknob, the soft stroke of wool, angularities and corners, globes of the world, plump strands of seaweed, the feel of a sculpture in a museum, and of

Wildly and delightedly dances

the next woman, every bit of her,

in her soft boots and her bordered

mantle, with jewels on her arms;

til one remembers the old dictum,

that every part of the body and

of the *anima* shall know religion,

and be in touch with the gods.[2]

D. H. LAWRENCE

course, the swell of my lover's breast or the curve of her thigh.

The kiss, our first intimate touch, begins with the feeding from our mother's breast; and from that early start, nourishment, aggression, comfort, and sexuality are all intermingled in the intimate pleasures of the mouth. A kiss can be an expression of desire, of friendship and greeting, of loyalty, or of spiritual blessing. A kiss can open the door to a person's heart; it can be a self-revelation; or as it was for Salman Rushdie, who grew up in India, it can be a simple way of honoring the world of everyday objects that we rely on:

> I grew up kissing books and bread. In our house, whenever anyone dropped a book or let fall a chapati . . . the fallen object was required not only to be picked up but also kissed, by way of apology for the act of clumsy disrespect. Devout households in India often contained, and still contain, persons in the habit of kissing holy books. But we kissed everything. If I'd ever dropped the telephone directory I'd probably have kissed that too. Bread and books: food for the body and food for the soul—what could be more worthy of respect than that?[3]

Rushdie's kisses were not sentimental; they were genuine expressions of regard for the world we live in. Neither Nature nor possessions need our sentimentality, our fantasies of what we think they are. They don't need us to foist some meaning on them that we may have lost in ourselves. What they do need is for us to give them the attention and respect due to them as part of the living world.

Wordsworth thought that Nature was a necessary second mother for the preadolescent child, and if that relationship was missing, the child's imagination would be stunted in some way in later life. Imagination, he would say, feeds on old tree roots, the smell of wet grass, the shimmer of corn in the sun.

Old tree roots in a rolling beech wood in upstate New York: I can sense it now, their musty, truffly smell reaching back into the more ancient regions of my brain. Smell has to be the most underrated of all our senses. We would be wise to let ourselves be led by the nose now and again. Smells inform our deepest instincts and intuitions, which is why we have expressions like "to smell a rat," "to smell an opportunity," or "to smell something fishy." In Inuit tribes the common greeting of rubbing noses has its basis in "smelling out" the intentions of others. In Asian countries like Borneo, Burma, and India the word for "kiss" also means "smell."

Everything we taste is snatched from death: our responsibility is to taste it completely.[4]

JOHN TARRANT

Smells can also serve to dredge up long-forgotten memories, and they do so because they are an essential component of our emotional "read" of a situation or a moment in time. Charles Dickens claimed that the merest hint of the type of paste used to fasten labels to bottles would plunge him into the anguish of his early years, when bankruptcy forced his father to abandon him in a warehouse where they made such bottles.

I had my own experience of the power of scent over memory when I was in Branscombe, one of those English villages that seems made for a picture postcard, all thatched roofs and little winding streets. I was walking past a cottage covered with roses and honeysuckle. I was about to lean into the roses when I suddenly caught the scent of something more humble. It was a faint tang, somewhat like pepper, not entirely pleasant but not unpleasant, either.

I turned my head. A pot of geraniums was hanging from the porch, and as I caught their smell, I instantly became eight years old again. On my way to school I would pick a leaf from the geraniums that hung over our neighbor's garden wall and enjoy the tingling sensation it sparked in my mouth. In that smell was the thrill of a private enjoyment, the pleasure of being out in the world on my own, in that exciting stretch of public domain that lay between the familiarity of home and the ordered safety of school.

Our sense of smell matters; it plays a large but usually unnoticed role in everyday decisions. It determines, often against all reason, our attraction or aversion to others. The male essential oil is androsterone. It smells approximately of musk, sandalwood, and a nuance of urine. Experiments have shown women selecting only the chairs, telephones, and theater seats that had been presprayed with this masculine odor. A woman smells sweetest and is thus most attractive during ovulation, when the rise in her blood sugar level adds to the sweetness of her breath.

Your lover's odor is certainly part of their attraction for you. That's probably why you like to wear his shirt or use his pillow when he is away, and why he is always sniffing your hair and around your neck. But we wouldn't want to go so far today as women did back in Elizabethan times. Then a woman would put a peeled apple under her arm for a while and offer the "love apple" to her beloved as a gift. Even Napoleon asked Josephine not to wash in the two weeks before they would next meet, so he could enjoy her natural perfume undiluted.

When we make love in the way Eve—who is the figure of the human soul—would have us make love, then not just our fingers but our toes and eyes and ears and every part and parcel of us is dancing to the thrill the laughter the tears the pathos the exquisite tenderness of being in such intimate communion with another human being. And because we have entered the world of time, we know that the first flushes of love can, in time, give way to the more sober work of forging an enduring relationship, which has its own pleasures, unknown to starry-eyed lovers. There is great pathos—a richness of feeling both poignant and passionate—in every transition from innocence to experience. What life wants of us, in all of our transitions, whatever they are, is that we feel it, all of it, whatever it is. Because the ability to be moved, to feel the bittersweetness of life in time, is the unique opportunity of being physical, one that an angel would give his wings for.

So our lovemaking does not have to be all thunder, lightning, and Beethoven to bring us the profound pleasure of being skin to skin in tender, vulnerable nakedness with another human being. What matters is that we are there, whatever is happening; that we can savor the scent of the other, follow the contours of their body with our fingers, let our eyes linger on them, and above all— greater than any technique, tantric or otherwise—offer them the gift of our presence: so simple yet so often elusive, the gift of just being there; being there, with and for the other, that is our deepest offering.

That is not so easy, though, when we confuse our fantasies and concepts about the physical world with the actual experience of it. To be in the world requires our whole body and mind. To be in the mind alone with our fantasies is to be in a world of our own and ultimately to be lonely. You might think, from the booming pornography business, that we live in the most sexually liberated culture of all time. But no, we live in a world of images; the erotic, on the other hand, is unmediated, directly relational.

Pornography is a caricature of the erotic; it can exist only by denying relationship. It demands anonymity. And without relationship there is no connectedness, nothing more than the tight circle of oneself. Instead of soul there is only sensation, which is only skin deep and for its own sake alone.

Pornography is the legacy of the religious fear of the flesh (of getting our hands dirty) and the split between body and soul. D. H. Lawrence was aware of this a long time ago. In *Women in Love*, Rupert Birkin says to Ursula:

"As it is, what you want is pornography—looking at yourself in mirrors, watching your naked animal actions in mirrors, so that you can have it all in your consciousness, make it all mental."

"But do you really want sensuality?" she asked.

"Yes," he said, "that and nothing else, at this point. It is a fulfillment—the great dark knowledge you can't have in your head—the dark, involuntary being. It is death to oneself—but it is the coming into being of another."[5]

The gustatory equivalent of pornography is fast food: quick, cheap, and convenient. But pleasure likes to take its time, especially when it comes to sex and a good meal. Slow is best when it's a matter of taking pleasure. Where else but in Italy would a Slow Food movement begin, which it has, in response to the ubiquitous demand for junk food that has penetrated even those bastions of culinary refinement, Italy and France. For the Slow Food movement, everything is in the preparation (as any good lover will know). You choose the ingredients not only for their freshness but for their variety of taste, color, and texture; you steam your vegetables to preserve their life juices; you cook everything over a low heat; you serve the result not all in one course but in two, three, or several; and you flavor the whole meal with leisurely conversation and appreciation of the surroundings. If you are serving lunch, you do not have an appointment before late afternoon—just like in the old days, at least around the Mediterranean.

It's an impossible way of life in today's world, you may say. But is it? Americans make fun of the French for having a thirty-five-hour workweek and five weeks' paid annual leave. How do they ever manage to run a functioning economy? Well, France happens to be the fourth largest economy in the world. The French also produce more per man-hour than do Americans. If they can do that and still take the time for a good meal and a good time, then perhaps the laugh is on us.

It was in France that I first learned the relationship of time to lunch. It was a Sunday in a small village on the edge of a gorge an hour inland from the Mediterranean. We had followed our noses and come to a small restaurant that had the air of a private house. To reach the dining room, you had to walk through a sitting room, complete with grandfather clock and three-piece suite. Inside, the six tables were packed with French families. The French love to eat out *en famille*, especially on Sundays. The pro-

prietor, an eager, wiry man with half a head of graying hair, beckoned us outside, where a single table was planted in the cobbled street.

We were the only tourists, this village being off the tourist route and still undisturbed by contemporary styles and affectations. Lunch was a set menu, the table was shaded by a large white parasol, and the street was silent. We sat down, returning the proprietor's smile.

Within a few moments he came running out with a huge bowl of coarse *pâté de campagne* held in a tight crust of butter. He set it between us with two formidable knives and some thick bread. He had two of these bowls, and they were passed from table to table as people came and went, though not many went. In the course of time we came to understand why.

We were encouraged to eat our fill and help it down with the *cocktail de maison,* a sparkling wine with real peach essence. In the shade of the parasol we sat and watched the fountain play and the bees swarm over the yellow roses climbing the wall opposite our table. Only a dog passed by in half an hour. We nattered contentedly for a while, taking more of the pâté than we normally would, in the absence of the appearance of anything else. The time eventually came when I could no longer resist looking at my watch. We had been there almost an hour already, and there had been no sign that anything was going to replace the pâté. Neither was there any sign of the *patron*.

I went to find him, and he looked at me with a mixture of embarrassment and incomprehension. He seemed not to understand the cause of my concern. Then he ran into the kitchen and came out with two more glasses of cocktail. *Compliments de la maison!* he beamed.

It was another full half-hour before the *confit de canard* arrived. In that half-hour we watched the dog scratch his ear with his hind leg; we wondered about the honeyed stone wall opposite, how long it had been standing, and the *lavoir* a few yards up the street, when women had last gathered there under its red tiled roof to chatter and rub and scrub their men's working clothes clean. And every now and then we wondered whether we should remonstrate any further about our fugitive *canard*.

When it came, stewed in its own juices, the most tender and delicate meat I have ever tasted, I knew that heaven was truly to be found on earth. All my concerns and growing indignation evaporated in the first flush of its fragrance, and time simply ceased to exist. Softened in body and mind by the sun, the cocktails, and the heavy pâté, warmed by the generosity of the portion, everything conspired to make us move slowly, each succulent mouthful interspersed with glances and grunts of approval and delight, with long looks at the roses, the stone, each other, everything entering our mouths in unison on the end of the fork.

As my duck disappeared from my plate, I felt gratitude for the *patron*'s complete lack of airs, for his absence of concern for my foreign haste, and for his instinctive capacity to serve food exactly as generations of men and women had done in that land before him.

This leg of duck falling away from its bone, its recipe had stood the test of decades of discerning French palates. And now we, who had dropped in from another world, were the benefactors of all that distilled knowledge and enjoyment.

When we finally embarked upon the sorbet dessert, it was almost four in the afternoon, but I would find it difficult to think of an afternoon more fruitfully, more pleasantly spent. The *patron* came out to join us for a final *digestif,* happy with his labors and the smiles on our faces, and I thanked him for helping me to learn to savor the passing of the hours.

Savoring, tasting, touching, hearing, seeing—these

are the gates through which the world pours in and through us. The wider we open those gates, the more fully we shall know the pleasures, unique to this embodied life, that are passing even now as we speak. And we shall come to this knowledge, not by hurrying to cram it all in, but by slowing down, so we may glimpse the vastness of every moment, every mouthful, every sight, sound, and touch of hand to hand as it happens.

I am not my fault. What it comes down to is that I am foolish because I am human, and the truth is that we are a species of fools. . . . I think the best thing for all humanity would be to celebrate our foolishness. Our most important holiday would then be April Fool's Day, one of the few festivals that celebrates all humanity, regardless of religion, skin color, nationality or political persuasion.[1]

WES NISKER

TWO

The Pleasure

of Being

Foolish

Falling in love is surely the most foolish and irresistible of all the pleasures available to any human being. Most of us fall for it at one time or another. My own story went this way: a fifty-three-year-old man sells his house in England, leaves a good but fading relationship of some thirteen years, says good-bye to his twenty-three-year-old son from an earlier marriage, and boards a plane for the United States and a new life. He has no idea what he is flying toward. All he knows is that he has a one-year visa and a book to write.

After two weeks in the Bay Area, where he has friends and an extended house-sit, he heads to Michigan for a month's retreat offered him by a foundation as a place to begin writing. Just before he leaves, the foundation calls to say they have double-booked their room for the first ten days of his stay, so they have arranged for him to stay for that time at another retreat center a short walk away over the hill.

When he arrives at this retreat center, which is a Mennonite one in a converted barn, he goes up to his room and immediately sits down to proclaim in his diary that this is the start of a whole new life. He can do anything, go anywhere, his life is an open book. The next day he goes down to lunch, which is held in silence, to discover there is only one other guest. He takes his plate and sits down in the place laid for him opposite her.

A woman. A woman sitting there with huge open eyes and a radiant smile. He smiles back, wanly, in astonishment. He doesn't know where to put himself. All he knows is that it's over. It's all over. The very last thing he

would ever have put in his diary, a gigantic love affair, has surged up out of nowhere and brushed every other option out of his mind.

He has just left a long relationship. He has barely spent more than a few months of his adult life without the intimate company of a woman; this would be his best opportunity ever to allow himself to enjoy his own company for an extended period, perhaps for the rest of his life. And what does he do? He falls in love within two weeks of leaving home. And with a woman nearly eighteen years his junior. It's all so predictable, you might say. And you would be right.

This alone would be enough to warrant an extended sigh. But that isn't the half of it. This woman, he discovers the very first day, is married with three children, two of them barely out of the toddler stage. Of course, to begin with he thinks that will let him off the hook. He gives a sigh of relief and over the first few days makes it clear that their emerging friendship must remain on a firmly platonic basis. But it doesn't happen that way.

A few days later he discovers she came to the retreat center already knowing that her marriage was over. They make love, but when, after ten days—yes, she was there for the exact same ten days—she leaves to go back home, neither of them speaks of any continuity. They never mention phone numbers.

Some weeks later I had an e-mail from Maria. She had noticed and remembered my address on my computer. It was a simple message inquiring about a church in New York I had mentioned, but it was an opener. We met three months later, and I discovered she was now divorced, and her children were in the primary custody of their father. Two years later we were married, with her two little girls as bridesmaids and her twelve-year-old son as best man. Five years later we are living in a house two blocks from her kids. Someone must be crazy, and maybe it's me. But I'm not about to become sane again anytime soon.

Love is a foolish pleasure indeed, because you can never fall in love and remain unscathed. You put your head on the block and have no idea whether you will remain in one piece. It just doesn't make sense. The Danish philosopher Kierkegaard suggested that "when two people fall in love and begin to feel they are made for one another, then they should break off, for by going on they have everything to lose and nothing to gain."

The Dane was a devout Christian who believed that love of God and neighbor were the only real loves, and that they were choices, which put them in a different category from the emotional, instinctual love that can arise un-bidden between two people. And yet even he knew we can often find ourselves between a rock and a hard place. "Fall in love with a woman and you will regret it. Don't fall in love with a woman, and you will regret it too," he said.

There is a whole chorus of voices down through the ages to prove him right, including the most renowned of all German literary figures, Goethe. He may have been the greatest sage of the eighteenth century, but even Goethe was willing to make a fool of himself for love. He was seventy-four when he fell hopelessly for Ulrike von Levetzow, a nineteen-year-old girl who perhaps sensibly declined his offer of marriage. In *The Marienbad Elegy*, Goethe describes in searing terms a heart breaking open:

> I have lost the whole world, I have lost myself—
> I who but lately was the darling of the gods. They
> put me to the test, they gave me Pandora with her
> abundant store of blessings and greater abundance
> of danger. They pressed me to the bountiful lips—
> they sunder me from them, and destroy me.

Kahlil Gibran must have known something of that pain. In *The Prophet* he writes,

For even as love crowns you, so shall he crucify you.
Even as he is for your growth so is he for your
pruning.[2]

And yet for every Goethe or Gibran there are ten poets who will declare there is no greater joy on earth than to fall in love. We know that love burns, but given the opportunity, we find it almost impossible to keep our hearts out of the fire. Whichever way we look at it, falling in love is surely a fool's game. It is the one arena of life where it is more obvious than anywhere else that you are not the one running the show. You can have no idea of the way it will all turn out, and you will be subject to all manner of emotions—doubt, fear, hope, ecstatic joy, jealousy, longing, rage—that you can only submit to, allow to pass, or savor while you can. And yet for all that, love is the deepest pleasure we can know on earth.

If you are in love you cannot help but throw caution to the winds. You cannot help but make decisions (you may seem to be choosing at the time, but more likely you are helpless to do anything else) that no sane person looking after their back would ever make, even on a bad day. And yet it is precisely in this abandonment that the profound pleasure of love, the joy of it, is to be found. Love is

If the fool would persist in his folly,

he would become wise.[3]

WILLIAM BLAKE

freedom from the known; it is freedom now, along with the intuition that ultimately you have nothing to lose anyway—only a string of gray days, a recurring sense of loneliness, and a life that, however fulfilling, probably doesn't quite add up.

The train of events set in motion by my marrying Maria has caused me to make a fool of myself in more ways than one. On our first family vacation from the United States to England, an old friend of mine invited us to join him on his boat on the River Dart, in Devon. My relationship with Maria's children was quite new, and I was naturally regarded with suspicion and reserve. To get to the boat, we had to row ourselves out for a hundred yards in a little dinghy. My friend took out the children and Maria, and his wife returned to the shore with the dinghy, leaving me to row out to the boat on my own while she went back to the house.

I know nothing about rowing and water currents, but it seemed a simple enough thing to do. The river was flowing gently, and my friend's wife had just arrived like an arrow at the shore. I headed toward the boat, but almost immediately began to drift downstream. I furiously paddled on the other side and somewhat righted my course but a little too much, so that the dinghy started to head upstream, parallel to the boat instead of heading toward it. I scrambled to adjust my course again, but despite my best efforts and barely thirty yards from my intended destination, the dinghy began slowly to rotate in circles.

I became aware that my wife and her three children were all looking on from the boat. I glanced up in embarrassment and strove even harder to bring the thing under control. My efforts only seemed to make matters worse. I sat there helplessly for a moment watching myself turn in circles.

I looked up at Maria and suddenly found myself laughing, laughing out loud. I held up the oars in a gesture of hopeless surrender to my predicament. The two girls started giggling, and a broad grin broke out on the older boy's face. In seconds everyone was doubled up in laughter.

In that instant my cover was blown. My need to appear capable, responsible, and manly was blown clean out of the water. The truth was revealed—that, faced with this simple task, I was nothing less than helpless and hopeless.

Yet in that moment I was able to meet those children in a way I had not done before. And my wife, too. Even with her—perhaps especially with her—I had been all too ready to confirm any notions she might have had about my wisdom concerning the ways of the world. I was the one with the life experience, the one who had done this and that, who had read and written the books and generally tramped about the world—a tale from which she has long since, of course, been disabused.

In truth, I couldn't even row a little boat in a straight line for a hundred yards. It was pitiful, really. But it was hilarious, too. And above all it left me undisguised, without a social mask, reduced to my bare essentials, which included my ineptness when faced with a simple task.

That's why it broke the ice with the children: they could see me now, in that moment, as a buffoon who was able to join in on the joke about himself, rather than as a threat to their relationship with their mother. It was a tiny, apparently insignificant moment, but it was the one that first began to cause a shift in our relationship. I was human, they realized, and, despite myself, funny with it, too.

Fifteen years earlier I had organized a trip for some twenty people to Ladakh, high in the Himalayas. It was advertised, and with good reason, as a real adventure. We would travel there by bus, over treacherous passes wide enough only for one-way traffic, and along which all the trucks and public buses, every one of them overloaded, had to chug.

As the road wound higher, I started getting headaches. A few days later, by the time we arrived in Leh, the capital of Ladakh, I was vomiting and could barely keep my eyes open. I had a severe case of altitude sickness. No one else had anything more than a slight headache. I was confined to bed on arrival and was unable to do much more than stagger around for the following week. This was not the kind of adventure that I had had in mind. My co-leader had to assume all responsibility for the group until just a few days before we left.

In the space of a few days I went from being the intrepid leader who led groups around the world to being the weakest link in the whole group, which was composed primarily of women. I had never been up in the mountains before, not that high. I assumed I would have no difficulty and took it for granted that I was perfectly qualified to head up a large group like this.

My usual terrain was desert or the African or Indian plains. At the time there were no effective medicines for altitude sickness, and the only thing I could do was to wait it out. It was impossible to pretend that I could cope, much less assume my leadership role, when everyone could see me flat on my back.

I felt utterly foolish and, at first, not in a good way. I was embarrassed, even ashamed of myself. But then individuals began to come to my room, give me water, rearrange my pillows, and tell me what they had done that day. I began to accept my condition: not just the sickness but the loss of my role and responsibilities and also of sharing the discovery of Ladakh with these people, all of whom were so eager and keen to explore.

I gradually began to see that I was receiving something else instead. Freed from my role—the image that I thought others wanted to see in me—I could relax into being my fallible and also vulnerable self, without any disguises. And because of that I was free to receive the warmth and the kindness of others. My incapacity seemed to kindle people's humanity and sense of community, not, as I had feared, their resentment. It could have happened to any of us, they would say. It could; but in the end, I was happy enough that it happened to me.

In both these instances, in Devon and in Ladakh, I became a fool despite myself. My foolishness returned me to my humanity and the humanity of others. It enabled me to be honest and authentic, free both of social constraints and any pretense of worldly wisdom. It especially encouraged me to lighten up.

It's not easy to lighten up when you have to seem to

know what you are doing: to be in control of yourself and of events. It's not easy to lighten up when every act has to have a purpose or a meaning. That's why, in my case, I have not often been a fool willingly. Usually, life has had to insist.

Maria seemed to know this about me from the start. As she was leaving the retreat center, she had given me a card. Inside, it said this:

Dear Roger,

My wish for you is this: do not deny yourself the magic and joy of a child. In all of your wisdom and wandering, make a place for the child within you. Rejoice in a piece of birthday cake on your birthday without concern for how it got there. That delightful innocence is in you too. I know.

Maria

I have often felt too busy to play, felt that important, meaningful issues are at stake, and that life is a serious business. It *is* serious, but not *that* serious. "Important" matters and issues, truth be told, matter most when my involvement makes *me* important—self-important, that is.

Being a fool lets the cat out of my bag, the wind out

of my sails. The word comes from the Latin *follis*, meaning "windbag, a pair of bellows." The pleasure of being foolish lies precisely in the freedom it gives from self-importance and social expectations; the freedom from striving, from the pressure to impress others, to do things the way others do them.

A fool is simply not responsible in the way most people are. He knows he is ultimately not responsible for the way things turn out. He isn't weighed down by the weight of the world. He knows the world won't descend into chaos if he takes a nap for half an hour.

I have never known a person so consciously foolish as Maria. She chose to accept just a few thousand dollars as a divorce settlement in her previous marriage and left the house, the pension, and both cars, which were all jointly owned, to her ex-husband. The clean break gave her a great deal more pleasure than the prospect of more money.

Then she spent the little money she did receive on allowing herself to do nothing for the year following her divorce. It would have been far more sensible to put a deposit down on an apartment or to find a way of earning an income, which, as a full-time mother, she had not done for twenty years. But no, the opportunity to let herself fall free of all her own as well as others' expectations, and to rest in the trust that she could let herself see what life might bring, was more important to her. Out of the blue, at the end of that year, when she was down to $300, she was offered a quarter of a million dollars for her first book. Who would have thought it!

Much to my dismay, and probably to your understandable disapproval, she has begun to smoke for the first time at the age of forty-two. She says she has felt like a smoker all her life but had never taken it up because of what people might think of her. For good or for ill, she now lives life on her own terms and not on the dictates of others. I don't like the smoking—I think it's downright crazy—but I respect her reasons for taking it up. And she enjoys it, her foolish pleasure.

She is a willing fool in other ways, too. She practices a generosity that I have still to learn or even fully understand. She regularly overtips both waitstaff and taxi drivers. "You don't need to give him that much," I often protest. "He probably earns more than you do. It only sets up expectations for other customers. It's not right. It's downright excessive. The whole tipping thing in this country is out of control anyway. In England you never give more than ten percent; in Europe, no more than twelve and a half. It's a proprietor's scam to avoid paying them a proper wage. It's outrageous. Not only that, the service isn't very good anyway!"

And on in that vein. She's heard it all before, and of course, she takes no notice. "This is my form of tithing," she says. "How would you like to wait tables or sit in traffic all day? It's tough work, and it serves the needs of people like you and me. A dollar more or less is not going to break me. It's just part of my way of giving back."

Who's right and who's wrong? That doesn't seem to be the appropriate question. But who has the most pleasurable, enriching experience of the same moment in time? I am taking the position of the worldly-wise, and I feel ripped off. She appears to be naïve and feels an appreciation for the person she is tipping. In that moment it is difficult to see how her moment is not richer than mine, even if it costs her a dollar more.

One of the most foolish virtues we can practice is generosity, especially when it means giving away something with no expectation of return. In a culture where profit-and-loss statements rule, it simply doesn't make sense.

A friend of mine recently asked a teenage boy if he might consider volunteering to work on a local housing project, helping to build homes for people on low incomes. "Why would I do that?" he scoffed. "Why would I work without being paid?" Why indeed! The mainstream culture he is growing up in provides him with no obvious reason. *Look out for number one* is the only attitude that seems to add up. Anything else would be foolish.

There are many forms of generosity, not just material, and one of them may be making allowances for a teenager's lack of experience regarding what really matters in this world. Giving room, the benefit of the doubt— this form of generosity doesn't require us to give away anything more than our suspicions, perhaps even our cynicism, about human nature.

But we hate the idea of being taken advantage of, having the wool pulled over our eyes. I do. I hate the idea I'm being taken for a ride. That's not making room for the fool in me; it's merely being stupid—and there's surely a difference.

Being the fool is not the same as acting the fool: you can't decide to be playful, or foolish, for an hour a day, as if it were yet another task to add to your campaign of self-improvement. It's rather the result of a relaxation of the rules and goals that you normally run your life by. A softening of the beliefs that hold up your world and your idea of who you think you are. The pleasure of foolishness lies in large part in the absence of self-consciousness; in the self-forgetting that comes in a moment of abandon.

Whenever I'm in a country where bargaining is the usual mode of transaction, I have enjoyed the poker game of going back and forth in order to walk off with my prize—a carpet, a painting, a piece of ceramic—for the lowest price possible. I would spend a day for the sake of reducing the price by the equivalent of five dollars. But more often than not I would walk away with not just my purchase but also with a tinge of regret. Sometimes I would feel downright mean.

There had to be a balance somewhere between walking off feeling I had been taken advantage of and walking away feeling strangely guilty. Then one day in Istanbul I fell instantly in love with a carpet in a small shop near the Topkapi Palace—right in the heart of the tourist district, where prices are always grossly inflated. The elderly vendor looked at the rug, flipped it over, and quoted a figure. I came back with something near half of his quote. He smiled and came up with a number somewhere between his and mine. I accepted without another word. It was all over in forty-five seconds. I was ecstatic as much for the ease, the simplicity of the transaction, as I was for the rug.

We both smiled, shook hands, and I walked out of that shop with my carpet and a light heart. For someone else, this would have been normal. For me, with my radar for being made a fool of, this was a breakthrough. A highly pleasurable one. And if I had been had, this time I truly didn't care.

We may run the risk of losing face or being taken advantage of in letting the fool in us have some say, but we may also be exposing ourselves to the possibility of genuine connection to other human beings; to the wisdom that comes from left field, synchronicity, and unlikely meetings on street corners. And you never know, we may even be opening the door to love.

If you lose your
sense of humor, it's just not
funny anymore.

WAVY GRAVY

We must be willing to let go
of the life we have planned
so as to have the life
that is waiting for us.

JOSEPH CAMPBELL

THREE

The Pleasure of

Not Knowing

We know a great deal. We know so much that we can be forgiven for thinking that with enough commitment, resources, and time, we shall eventually solve every human problem and crack every code that nature has to offer. We shall be as gods walking the earth. As we pursue the science of genetics, cloning, and brain stem research, it will surely be only a matter of time before the secret of life itself will be ours.

All of which only adds to the aura and primacy of knowledge, the power and the glory of it, the delight of it and the greed for it. Which in turn is why parents spend a fortune sending their kids off to college. We like to know because knowledge seems to give us control—over ourselves, our future, our environment, and perhaps, eventually, even over death.

Knowledge is a wonderful thing. It can help you earn a good living, gain status, and assume authority. But the known is already explored territory. How interesting would it be to live in a world in which everything is known and under control? There would be no amazement, no wonder, no edge. Everything would run according to plan, and our own lives would play out like clockwork. There are people who live lives like that today.

I used occasionally to go to clairvoyants. Sometimes they would tell me things that turned out to be true. Like I would meet a girl, and buy a house in November. But the trouble with knowing the future—assuming that what you think you know turns out to be true—is that you don't really have a future anymore. Because if you know what's going to happen, it becomes no more than an extension of

An act of pure attention,
if you are capable of it,
will bring its own answer.[1]

D. H. LAWRENCE

your life as you already know it. In a way, it's already happened. It leaves you with no room to maneuver. It certainly leaves you without much choice. If we know the future, we can only live through a program, which isn't quite the same as a life and is certainly a lot less fun.

Being human, however, it's a life that we have, which means that any given moment can offer a vivid aliveness that no amount of knowledge or information can provide. This moment is inherently unknowable, and it's when we are fully immersed in it that life feels really worth living.

Take this very moment, for example, the one in which you are reading these words. You turn to look and it's gone. And yet when can revelation—a sudden opening of our mind and eyes—happen if not now? And Now. When it comes to living, the moment we are in is the only one with genuine promise. This very moment is precisely the one we can't plan for. Here it is, and it's gone before we know it. The only thing we can do is to live it, embody it, rather than what I find myself doing all too often, which is to think about it when it is already too late.

Any moment can take us by surprise, if we are open to surprises. Yet the moment we first open our eyes in the morning can seem more accessible than most. In this moment, there is a window, a brief opening when the world can be seen fresh and new without the stream of opinions and ideas that kick in a moment later about everything we have to do as soon as we get up.

This morning I awoke, and instead of rolling automatically out of bed to check my e-mail, I let my eyes linger on what lay before them: a zigzag of blue on a corner of my duvet three inches from my nose. In a fold of cloth, a few inches away, I could make out the flesh of my wife's upper left arm. White, with a flush of pink and brown, a beautiful tenderness. I could not see where this hint of a human being had come from, nor where it was going. Only that it was there, moist and humming with a large life all its own. Questions began to drift through the sky of my mind. *Who is this person lying beside me?* I wondered. *Where did she come from, and how did she come to be here? How did I come to be here?* I realized then that I truly do not know this person at all. I have lived with her for some years now; I have looked often upon her face and felt more than once an upwelling of joy. But she is more of a mystery to me today than she ever was.

Even in our first moment of meeting there was some hint of familiarity, some sense of recognition, but now, more often than not, when I look at her going about her day, I realize she is utterly unknown to me. Not in a way that implies disconnection or remoteness, as in "They have become strangers to each other." No, in the way that I think Gabriel García Márquez meant when he said of his wife, "I know her so well that she is completely and utterly unknown to me."

The person we live with is one of the great unknowns in our life. To see them without preconceptions, in their mysteriousness, is to see them for themselves, rather than as some appendage to our own lives. And that can bring pleasure not only to us but also to them. It is liberating to be seen for who we are, an ungraspable complexity rather than a predictable list of characteristics. Clear seeing like this can even rejuvenate a flagging love.

There I go again, already off on a whole train of thought about famous authors, love, and my lover's arm, and the moment has evaporated; but then I become aware of my own arm, lying languid on top of the covers. And the sight of that arm brings me back to the body lying next to the woman in the bed. My body. Whose body? This humming life's body. This tingling, breathing, fleshy, thinking, wondering creature lying here—who, and what, *is* this, lying here with my name attached to it?

The one thing that I, like most of us, want to appear

certain of is myself. What a paradox, then, that I'm the subject that I seem to know least about! Though I can tell you what I do and where I live and am intimately acquainted with a string of personal characteristics, annoying or otherwise, the person who looks back at me in the mirror is an unfolding mystery, not a static portrait to be captured in glass, words, or anything else. In fact, despite my strong opinions about most things from dinner to the state of the world, it has gradually come to my attention over the course of a lifetime that I'm not the only subject I know so little about.

When I turn to face it, I can only acknowledge the fact that what I like to think I know is in a way already obsolete. Because facts are in themselves dead things. Life is constantly shifting from moment to moment. And if we are in the flow of it, we won't have any attention or breath left over for explanations. It's only when we step back from life and from our experience, back into the somewhat lonely position of the observer, that we feel inclined to voice an opinion. But by then life has moved on and we are already out of the picture.

All I know, lying in this bed or not lying here, is that this is the life that was given to me. The life that throbs along through any and all of my moments: this is it! If ever I wonder what my life was meant to look like, I have only to look around me. This, whatever I am doing or not doing, is what it is. This, right here, is as good as it gets! Your "one wild and precious life,"[2] as Mary Oliver says. And when you follow its movement, without trying to direct it with preconceived plans for the future, your life will lead you where you need to go. When you trust it, your body, rather than your mind, will walk you through the life you are meant to be living, whatever it may be.

In its best moments, this is what writing feels like to me. My brain follows the dance of my fingers, not the other way around. I see what's on the page to find out where I'm going. As to why I write at all, that is another question I have no answer for. I can only think it's a personal neurosis, all those words on the page seeming to fill up the blank space. I just can't help doing it. It's a tic, though a pleasurable one. It's just what I do, and the funny thing is, the less I know what I am going to say, the more enjoyable the experience is.

The brain following the lead of the fingers in writing is the kind of intentionality that allows us to cooperate with life instead of trying to control the outcome in advance. In her own book, *Caught in the Act*, my editor,

Toinette Lippe, captures this wonderfully. She is a student of Chinese brush painting, and she says that

> the secret is just to move the brush and watch what happens as it happens. Observe the energy moving. Holding onto an idea of where you want to go puts a strain on the way in which you move, and the strokes you make while under the influence of this idea come in little lurches.[3]

So the pleasure of not fully knowing where you are going or why doesn't mean you merely drift through life like a leaf in the wind. The fact that we can never see the whole picture doesn't mean we don't bother to form any personal intention—it acknowledges that our intention is best served by an open, attentive mind, one that is receptive and cooperative with the larger forces of life around it, whatever they may be. Then life can be what it is, a mystery, and not just an agenda; a mystery that is constantly revealing itself, and of which we are a part, instead of an agenda we have to laboriously work through. Life as revelation is a pleasure indeed.

One of the times I had a taste of what it was like to lose my agenda was when I couldn't find the exit to the

maze at Hampton Court, the palace outside London where King Henry VIII spent much of his time. It's not an especially large maze, though large enough to get lost in, I discovered, with its high hedges and clever blind alleys. I went in thinking it would be a few minutes of pleasant diversion, but after ten minutes of going in circles I realized it was rather more complicated. I came to a standstill somewhere in the middle—at least, that is where I thought I was—and realized that the aim I had come in with, which was to walk through and out, had evaporated. In its place was simply the sensation of myself going nowhere. For a moment I was returned to a simple, primal innocence. There are few experiences more pleasurable than that.

Perhaps, if the maze had been larger and there was no one to call out to, I would have felt trapped and afraid. But no; I felt nonplussed, a pleasant sensation of free fall, suspended somehow from the life I normally identified as mine. And I understood in that moment the deeper purpose of mazes. Yes, it was fun for the aristocracy to play at being lost in their formal back gardens, but their true purpose, it dawned on me, is to a-maze us. It even gave us the word. *Amazing.* The exit, I discovered when I started walking again, was less than a minute from where I had been standing.

What are mazes, or labyrinths, after all, if not a metaphor for life? We often find ourselves retracing our steps, getting lost, and even coming upon the exit sooner or later than we imagined. Life can indeed be a-mazing. And, as in a maze, the next step can be much closer than we imagine, and often in a direction we would never have suspected. This was just how it felt the moment I left England for America. Boarding that plane to a new life, I felt like the proverbial goat in midair between two cliffs. I took the leap without having any idea where, or even if, I was going to land. I was filled with a sense of risk and opportunity all at the same time. I had never felt more alive; and I certainly never dreamt I would land in a love affair.

But that plane ride was a rare occasion. Most of the time, I act as if I know what I am doing, as if I were on solid ground. After all, we are born into a culture that is founded on the premise that we should know what we want and go after it in such a way as to realize it. This, in essence, is the beauty of the American Dream. You can do it if you really want to. You can have it if you really want it. People come from all over the world to be able to act out their own version of the same dream.

And dreams can indeed come true. Our plans may work out just the way we wanted; our learning may bring us much comfort. Having an eye on the future is no bad thing. In its own way, it can be a wonderful thing. It can feel good to be in control of your life, to know where you are going and achieve your goals.

It can feel good because it makes us feel solid and safe. But isn't it true that the safer we become the more safe and secure we want to be? You make a million, and you want two. Because what we want to ensure is our future. We want to know that we *have* a future, because we can sense those shifting sands beneath our feet. We are afraid we may not last, and with good reason, since there is plenty of evidence to confirm our fears. That's worrying. It's enough to give anyone tight shoulders, a stiff neck, and a nasal voice.

We are the only creatures on earth with a word for tomorrow, and tomorrow exerts a very strong pull—at least, it has done on me. It gives me the comforting sensation that I am not going to disappear anywhere anytime soon, if ever. It assures me I have a life ahead of me—things to do, places to go, and knowledge to gain. Good old me— the one with the worn overcoat in the closet and the pair of brown shoes that need polish—will just soldier on, come what may, writing my way on into the future as if I know what's what.

The trouble is, it just won't wash. Nothing I do or know or write can save me. We are asking for the impossible when we ask for security. Security just doesn't exist. Not in life, anyway, because full security requires us to be immune to change. Even a stone statue doesn't get that guarantee. Michelangelo's *David* doesn't look quite the same now as he did to his maker. One day a few hundred years ago someone threw an object out of a window and took a chip out of him. Even if you are David, you just never know.

And yet not knowing can be a pleasure, because it gives you your life back. It returns us to essentials because it's actually our essential condition: we don't even know what the next moment will bring, not to mention the bigger issues of who started this whole show in the first place, how it will all end, or when our own curtain will finally fall. We just don't know. No wonder we wonder.

Have you ever wondered, for example, about beauty? What it is, why it impresses us so, and whether it is only in the eye of the beholder? There are art historians who labor for years to understand a single painting. They may come to know everything there is to be known about it and yet still not be able to explain the impact of its beauty.

In the Cloisters, a branch of the Metropolitan Museum in New York City, hang the seven tapestries known as *The Hunt of the Unicorn,* woven at the end of the fifteenth century in Brussels. They are considered the most remarkable and beautiful tapestries in existence, though their meaning remains largely uncertain.

The curator of the Cloisters, Timothy Husband, has looked at these tapestries almost every day for thirty-five years. "Sometimes," he said in an interview for *The New Yorker,* "I come in here and try to pretend I have never read anything about them. But it's not easy to shed that baggage. And my other reaction, sometimes, is just to say, 'To hell with it, someday someone will figure them out.' And then I find a solace in their beauty, and I can stare at them in pure amazement."

Standing amazed like the curator—standing before any ordinary moment awake and receptive without preconceptions—is rather like sneezing, or yawning. In those seconds when our mouth is wide open without words coming out of it, we are defenseless. We are just there in our native simplicity, with none of our learned ways of presenting ourselves to the world. We are tender and open. We are who we are.

One of the times that I have known such a pleasure

is when I first looked up at the retreat center in Michigan and came eye to eye with Maria. I had no name for the sensation, other than, perhaps, *dumbstruck*. When we are wordless—which is probably a condition for falling in love—and especially when our jaw is dropped, another kind of aliveness can swoop in and scatter all our preconceptions and carefully laid plans.

One invitation to such aliveness is an attitude of curiosity. Curiosity causes us to wonder. Wonder causes us to gape. We can no longer keep such a tight hold on life when, just as in yawning, our mouth is wide open. The more I have come to realize how little I know of this life, the more curious I have grown. If we are curious, we at least know that our heart is still beating. Curiosity opens doors and connects us to the larger life of the world. It is a key as much to this moment as to some grand project that can last a lifetime. It allows us to follow our nose, and there's pleasure in that. We wonder what lies around the corner or over the hill; we wonder what the empty canvas, the unhewn block of stone, conceal that our imagination may reveal. We wonder about that man, or that woman, we saw on the subway.

Curiosity tends to close down, and life becomes far more predictable, if you fence yourself in with a firm

"You talked about the first
principle again, but I still
don't know what it is,"
I said to Suzuki.
"I don't know," he said,
"*is* the first principle."[4]

DAVID CHADWICK, ON SHUNRYU SUZUKI

set of beliefs. Religious beliefs, beliefs we have about ourselves, about others, about life, construct the world as we know it. They are the stories we tell to make sense of our lives, to give meaning and continuity to our idea of who we are. Our stories tend to make us feel safe. They comfort us with the idea that we know—that we know what we are here for, who others are, and where we are all going after this ends. We all have beliefs, and we probably can't do without them. But if they run our lives, nothing will be a surprise. We shall live under the weight of our own preconceptions. Wonder will be a thing of the past, and life will likely grow more somber.

It would surely be a more pleasurable existence if we held beliefs the way scientists do their theories: as working models that serve while we continue to wonder and question and that are replaced when we reach another, more accurate working model.

If, say, you believe in past lives or in heaven or hell, chances are you do so not from direct experience, but from the authority of religious establishment. They are hand-me-downs that have been passed on from generation to generation. How do we know if we have lived many lives, or if we are going to go to heaven or hell, or if either of

A plague upon it!
I have forgot the map!

these even exists? If you are a Buddhist, you will believe in one outcome, and if you are a Christian, you will believe in the other. So who's right?

Generally, we don't know. The answer may well be both, but the point is this: if we live our lives by the dictates of received wisdom alone, we close the door on inquiry and wonder. We are closing the door on our own minds, all in the name of reducing the living mystery of life itself to an accessible formula that makes us feel safe.

Beliefs give us working models through which to engage with the world. In this way, they are useful. But when they exist merely to shore us up, to stave off our insecurity, they prevent us from being fully alive. The more fluid we allow our beliefs to be, the more we are prone to curiosity and even awe. The truth of our situation is that we don't know what this is. We don't know what the next moment of our life may bring. Each and every one of us is a living wonder.

How much more of a mystery, then, is the great circle of life itself? The spiritual, as distinct from the religious, is the indefinable, living spirit that moves through all things. And because spirit is living, it can never be contained in a set of commandments.

That can be scary and also amazing. Both. If we are willing to immerse ourselves in the living stream, the less we shall know about the truth of who we are or who anyone else is or what the meaning of it all is, and the more delight we may begin to feel in all of it. In the unexpected, the unimagined, the unthinkably complex dance of it all. Except we don't. Certainly I don't. Well, not always. Not even often. But it happens, and I am thankful enough for that, for those fleeting, wakeful moments of beauty and truth. They are the real joy of being human, brief matches that flare in the dark.

A week before she died, at the age of eighty-two, I asked my mother if there was anything she wanted to pass on to me: any thought on living or dying that she might want to leave to the next generation. She looked up at me from her hospital bed, all large eyes gazing out at me from gaunt features. I shall never forget that look. She reached out her hand and, with a faint smile, gripped my arm. I shall not forget that either. In her dying hours, my mother communicated to me not what she knew but who she was.

The willingness to let go of what we know you might even call an expression of faith. Faith: not that things will work out as we hope, but faith, simply, in life and its extraordinary intelligence that never fails to surprise. While belief holds on tightly, faith lets go. Lets go of the known and the predictable and offers itself to what cannot be grasped or even understood: this wild, impossible, wonder-ful life-as-it-is.

The capacity to tolerate complexity and welcome contradiction, not the need for simplicity and certainty, is the attribute of an explorer.[5]

HEINZ PAGELS

Imperfections unique to every microchip can be used to make them impossible to clone.[1]

NEW SCIENTIST

FOUR

The Pleasure

of Not

Being Perfect

Now that I look at it, someone else would probably have work done on a nose like mine. It's a significant promontory with a bump in the middle, what you might call a signature nose, inherited from my father. There's no doubt there are better-formed noses, but it would never occur to me to alter mine. It's not that I like it; it's that I've never really given it the time of day, except on the rare occasions it takes on a reddish hue and begins to sniffle. Perhaps I would think differently if it were hooked, crooked, or otherwise bent out of shape. But as an ordinary example of a large olfactory, it does not, in my opinion, need improving upon.

When it comes to the belly—my belly, that is—there has always been a slight protuberance for as long as I can remember. A little more than slight, perhaps. I eat well, mindfully that is—lots of avocado, lettuce, wild salmon, and chocolate mousse. When I forgo the latter for a while, the rise seems to subside, though never for too long. I concluded years ago that this gentle bulge is part of the Housden shape. This Housden's shape, anyway. It's great to feel lithe, but a good mousse now and then is perhaps marginally better. It just doesn't seem to make sense to deprive myself of such a genuine pleasure. There's great satisfaction to be found in a little of what you fancy, my father would say, and I would agree. Too much would be going too far, though, whatever too much is.

Today noses and bellies are routinely smoothed out all over the world, while other areas of the anatomy are as routinely buffed up and amplified. Very few of us are perfect specimens of the human form. We all have our physical imperfections, and many of them we share with most everyone else. Breasts are too small, thighs are too thick, cheeks are too plump, there's always something not quite right. That's generally how it is with the human body: not quite right.

So if you don't like the body you have, you can, as Michael Jackson did, go so far as to change it almost beyond recognition. And you will soon be able to beef up those muscles without going to all that effort in the gym. A boy was born three years ago whose upper arm muscles were abnormally large. By the age of two he could lift weights that would be a stretch for a ten-year-old. Curious scientists discovered he has a gene that most people don't. It isn't any longer science fiction to suggest that within a few short years that gene will be transferable to other newborns.

You can just as easily change your mind as you can your body. We already have pills for memory, but it won't be long before you can download Google directly into your brain. A Google implant is definitely on the way. Welcome to the world of the enhanced human being. Botox and Viagra will seem quaint in a few years' time. Perhaps the gym membership will seem quaint as well. After all, if you can get the results without all the sweat, then why not pay up and have yourself biochemically and genetically tuned?

Not that our urge to become an improved model is anything new, or merely another sign of Western civilization's general decline: the desire for self-improvement is as old as the human race. Young Greeks were working out two and a half thousand years ago. Montaigne wrote of French women in the sixteenth century that he had

> seen some of them swallow sand and ashes, and work deliberately to ruin their stomach, so as to get pale complexions. To get a slim body, Spanish style, what torture do they not endure, tight-laced and braced, until they suffer great gashes in their sides, right to the live flesh—yes, sometimes even until they die of it?[2]

Then think of all those monks in the desert in the first few centuries after Christ, twisting their bodies and minds into contortions in their attempts to climb a ladder to heaven. We have always felt less than perfect in one way or another, and we probably always will. Even when we have got the best body we could ever hope for; even when, a few years from now, we can buy a memory chip at Radio

Shack, or have surgery for a muscle gene, a math gene, or some other enhancement gene (it's not if, it's when), the feeling that we are incomplete will not go away.

It won't go away because it comes with the package of being human. It's in our hard drive. Something always seems to be missing, even if we can't put our finger on it. Because it's not easy to identify, we often blame it on conditions. We aren't earning enough, we don't have the right partner, we are in an East Coast winter when we could be sitting in the warmth of California. But we earn more, we change partners, we go to California, and though life may be more comfortable and warm—and there's no denying the consolation in that—the itch for something more or different remains the same.

So we meditate, we go into therapy, we take classes to improve our sex lives, we read books on how to find our vocation and "follow our bliss." But while any or all of these strategies may have genuine benefits, none of them will fix the underlying problem, because the problem is not fixable. It is part and parcel of the human story. Ultimately, working on yourself—trying to change the basic program—doesn't really work, because limitation, imperfection, is built into our genetic code.

In a results-driven culture like ours, a suggestion like

I too knitted myself the old knot of
  contrariety,
Blabb'd, blush'd, resented, lied, stole, grudg'd,
Had guile, anger, lust, hot wishes I dared not
  speak,
Was wayward, vain, greedy, shallow, sly,
  cowardly, malignant,
The wolf, the snake, the hog, not wanting
  in me.[3]

WALT WHITMAN

this borders on heresy. We tend to assume that every problem has a solution if only we persist and use the right tech-
nology. And in a global culture we can search for solutions
all over the planet. If it's self-knowledge we need, the
Tibetans, for example, must know what's what. They have
developed technologies of the mind for over a thousand
years. Or Zen monks from Asia. Surely they can help us
on our way.

Of course they can. But they may not lead us where
we think we want to go. In the end every tradition that
specializes in the spiritual welfare of human beings seems
to have one teaching in common. Christian, Buddhist,
Muslim, Jew—all agree that, ultimately we can only bow
our heads to the fact of our limitations and to the mystery
of existence. They would echo the words of the poet T. S.
Eliot when he said that

The only wisdom we can hope to acquire
Is the wisdom of humility: humility is endless.[4]

If you look at the self-help best-seller list, however,
you will find it full of titles like *Ask and It Is Given;*
Manifest Your Destiny: Nine Spiritual Principles for Getting
Everything You Want; The Magic of Believing; and *The*

Spontaneous Fulfillment of Desire. I have read none of these books, and they may well contain wisdom that I am in need of myself. But their titles lead me to suspect that these authors are peddling the magical thinking of a five-year-old as a cure for the adult's longing for the perfect life. As if a life worth living depended on the fulfillment of all our desires.

Humility brings us down to earth and lets us acknowledge our true condition, which is that we are flawed and were never meant to be otherwise. The perfection fantasy exists to shore up our illusion of having some control over a life that will never, in reality, conform to our plans.

Whatever technical wizardry we have at our disposal, however sophisticated our spiritual practices, we shall never get to the bottom of who we are, never uncover all our fault lines and layers of subtle unrest. These are puzzles that will remain as ungraspable and nebulous as ever, just like the puzzle of life and death. That is their beauty, and our beauty, too: we will always be just beyond our own grasp. There's great pleasure in accepting that we are fine just as we are, cracks and all.

Since we're not perfect, we can be pretty sure that we make mistakes. However responsible and cautious we may be, mistakes still happen anyway. If you are human, they are unavoidable. We take the wrong job, we choose the wrong partner, we bet on the wrong horse, we buy when we should have sold, we have one drink too many. But mistakes rarely seem like mistakes at the time. Only with hindsight can they take on the appearance of errors of judgment.

Can we ever be sure that mistakes are really mistakes? After all, we can never fully know the true outcome of any course of action. It's not just a matter of the obvious fact that mistakes give us opportunities to learn—a point famously reputed to have been made by Thomas Edison, the "Wizard of Menlo Park" who, after years of failed experiments to produce a lightbulb, said, "I haven't failed. I've found ten thousand ways that don't work." But there may even be a deeper elegance latent in error: the idea that whatever we may or may not have done, all of it goes toward making the person we are. Any apparent wrong turn can have surprising and joyful consequences that we could never have foretold at the time. The point is, we just never know; we never know where our blessings will come from or how it will all turn out.

Perhaps, given the forces at play both within and around us at any given moment, we only ever do the best we can, even if we are able to make a wiser choice in the very next moment. The inner weather can change faster than a spring day in New York. And who would deliberately set themselves on a course that they know to be wrong? Perversity exists, certainly, but its very name places it in a class of its own. Mistakes, if they can be called such, come with the territory of being human.

If we are not willing to acknowledge mistakes, and if we insist on appearing to get it right in all that we do and seem to be, we set ourselves up to become spiritual materialists, misapplying the rules of material progress to the inner worlds of psyche and spirit in our desire to perpetuate ourselves—to put a good (calm) face on it for as long as we're here, and to chalk up brownie points for the hereafter.

My wife spent years in her previous marriage trying to be the perfect mother, and it nearly killed her. As a culture, we spend a great deal of energy and money trying to fix ourselves according to some prevailing model—cultural, religious, or otherwise—of how we should be shaping up. We become our own project. Faust took that route as far as it goes; so did Dr. Frankenstein; and we all know what happened to them.

Some of us, including me, have spent years building a persona out of our idea of what a "conscious" life should

The Enhanced are people who love the idea of thinking faster, living longer, remembering everything, connecting to everything, staying muscular, conquering disease, being sexy forever. They will pay almost any price for that kind of transformation. The Enhanced are those who, through modifications to their minds, memories, metabolisms and personalities, can perform feats so unattainable by original-equipment human beings as to draw attention to themselves.

The Naturals are those who have access to those opportunities, but pass them by, like vegetarians shunning meat. For aesthetic, moral, or political reasons, they recoil in horror from the consequences, especially the unintended ones. Naturals are original-equipment humans who have the opportunity to become Enhanced, but have turned against it.

The Rest are those who, for economic or geographic reasons, do not have access to these technologies. They envy and despise those who do. The Rest are original-equipment humans with no choice to become Enhanced.[5]

JOEL GARREAU

look like. Most of my adult life has been spent in the company of others who share my views. We all agree that you'd be a fool not to eat organic food when you have the choice, to smoke, to watch television soaps, and to eat ice cream in bed. It only makes sense to read uplifting books, to meditate, to work through your neuroses with a therapist, to practice yoga or tai chi.

Only since I have known Maria—the only intimate person in my life who did not see the world through the same lens as me—have I started to realize the extent to which, the whole while, and largely unknown to myself, I had been growing a "spiritual" ego that was threatening to marginalize anything that didn't fit into its picture of how things should look.

It's not, of course, that there is anything intrinsically wrong with my preferences. It's that my preferences had constellated into an idea of myself that was largely self-satisfied and more than a little full of itself. After all, I thought I knew what was what. I had read the right books, traveled to all the right places, met the right people, and had had more than a few moments of clarity and insight, all of which my ego had duly appropriated. And an ego is an ego—a false self—however conscious it might appear. Maria, on the other hand, breaks all the rules. Life with her has loosened my grip on the way I think things ought to look and to be. She goes to no classes, studies no texts, eats what she wants and when; she reads the gossip columns, and she doesn't meditate. So where does her clarity and wisdom, so evident to anyone in her company, come from? She would say only that she loves God in her moment-to-moment experience and is devoted to watching the movement of her own mind. She has shown me that a person's preferences and beliefs are not a measure of who they are; that a far surer guide is how spacious, nonjudgmental, and inclusive a person is—first, of all the different parts of themselves and then, by extension, of others. You know when you are in the presence of someone like that. You don't want to leave them.

It is a consolation to come together with others of like mind, and to have our beliefs confirmed by them. A sense of belonging can alleviate our restlessness and sense of lack. In any event, the biochemists will say, restlessness is likely to be the result of a serotonin deficiency. That's one way to look at it, and we shall indeed feel more at ease with ourselves—less irritable, impulsive, and anxious—if we boost our serotonin levels by giving up the sugars for the complex carbs. We can definitely fix many mood swings and stress with intelligent dietary and exercise de-

There is a crack, a crack in everything.
That's how the light gets in.[6]

LEONARD COHEN

cisions, and with the application of our knowledge of brain chemistry.

But chemistry is not all we are. For the great majority of us, restlessness, a sense of lack and separation, is intrinsic to being human. When I am in New York, I wonder about Paris. When I am in Paris, I think of London. In London I think of my friends in New York. I shall probably always hear whispers leading me to suspect there might be something greener elsewhere. Show me a map of the Mediterranean, and all my longings flutter up like sand swallows.

But it has gradually dawned on me that my dreaming is an intrinsic part of who I am; it has caused me as much joy as it has trouble, so why would I want to change it, much less get rid of it, any more than I would the nose on my face? Why would I deprive myself of the poignant pleasure of nostalgia? Trouble comes, not when the itch starts to itch, but when I persist in trying to scratch it away; in trying to do something to fix it.

On those occasions when I allow myself simply to feel my longing, say, for Paris, I realize that the energy in my restlessness is nothing other than my own life energy rising in temperature; and as I let the intensity grow, I even begin to break out in joy instead of in a rash of envy toward those who are already strolling along the Seine. What I'm wanting from Paris, or wherever it is, is not Paris—that's only the image my desire comes dressed in. What I'm wanting is the very thing I already have, I realize; this warmth inside my chest that my nostalgia for Paris has spawned. If I let them, Paris, London, and Rome can take me back to myself, and that is a genuine pleasure. This is what the old Sufi poet, Rumi, meant when he said

This longing
You express is the return message.[7]

Wise counsel, but you have to be ready to hear it. It didn't stop me spending decades running around the globe looking for my own shadow. If you had asked me, I might well have been self-important enough to say I was a spiritual seeker—a respectable enough identity to be going along with at the time. At least I was *something*. Just not, it turns out, quite who I thought I was, some special case deserving of rare insight. But that's okay. It was as good a ride as any, and the bumps in the road loosened me up a little, knocked some of my spots off.

We're not perfect, but neither is there anyone out there more perfect than we are. What a pleasure this realization is! We are no more and no less than wonderfully ordinary, imperfect mortals. So why not give ourselves a break? Why not celebrate our blemishes, our imperfections, as the very qualities that make us human? No one else has quite our mix of idiosyncrasies. We all have a fault line, and usually one with many branches. It will always be that way, as it always has. Even mighty Achilles had his heel. And doesn't Venus de Milo look better without her arms? Both Nietzsche and Hitler were obsessed with the Superman ideal, and it didn't exactly take them in the direction they were hoping for.

As long as our habits do no harm to ourselves or to others, there is no reason to consider them anything less than our own unique contribution to global diversity. Instead of apologizing, we can choose to enjoy ourselves just as we are, no upgrades necessary.

It can get complicated, of course, when you are in a relationship, especially if you are sharing a life with someone. How do you do what you want to do, live as you want to live, when your ways run contrary to those of your partner? Robert Bly has this to say:

The inner nest, not made by instinct
Will never be quite round,

And each has to enter the nest
Of the other, imperfect bird.[8]

Our partner's imperfections come with the relationship package, just like our own. But only when we can acknowledge ours shall we be able to free them of our
criticisms. It has taken me a long time to see the ways I
have hidden a sense of lack beneath a suave and confident
exterior. It is precisely because they triggered my own
sense of inferiority that I judged some of Maria's lifestyle
choices to be inferior and less "conscious" than my own.
Only when I finally saw this did my judgments of her fall
away.

Not being perfect allows us to feel empathy and compassion, not just for ourselves but also, and especially, for
others. We see our own frailties and shortcomings in our
friends and lovers, or we see that they stumble in their own
way just as we do in ours. Not being perfect together joins
us in our humanity. That's a good feeling, that we're all in
this impossible, crazy life together, and that in large measure it will take us where it wants to go. That may cause
anxiety to our control needs, but it beats being lonely in a
posture of having it all together when everyone around
you seems (in your view) less than capable.

For all their massed omniscience
and omnipotence . . . the gods themselves
lost at Ping Pong, choked on the big
points, and suffered from back trouble
and the thousands of other aches and
pains—pulled muscles, sprained ankles,
colds   that the flesh is heir to.[9]

GEOFF DYER

In Japan there is an entire worldview that appreciates the value of the imperfect, unfinished, and faulty. It's called Wabi Sabi, where the first term refers to something simple and unpretentious, and the second points to the beauty that comes with age. Wabi Sabi is the aesthetic view that underlies traditional Japanese art forms like the tea ceremony, calligraphy, and ceramics. It's an aesthetic that sees beauty in the modest and humble, the irregular and earthly. It holds that beauty comes with the patina of age and in the changes that come with use. It lies in the cracks, the worn spots; in the green corrosion of bronze, the pattern of moss on a stone. The Japanese take pleasure in mistakes and imperfections.

In the West no one more than Rembrandt took such pleasure in painting old people. He painted them from the time he was twenty until the month before he died. Young people didn't interest him as models—probably because a young face, even if beautiful, does not have the passage and mark of life upon it. Age spots, wrinkled hands, the lines of experience, the lifetime you can see in an older person's eyes—these always fascinated him more than the untested beauty of youth.

Day by day tiny specks of us float away. No matter which exercise or diet regimen we follow, no matter which self-help guru we believe in, nothing will dispel the reality that we are not built to last. Death is our supreme limitation, the final proof that perfection was never meant to be part of the human experience. A hundred years from now, all new people. Sooner rather than later, we shall not be here: no eyes, no nose, no ears, no tongue, no mind; no you or me; gone, who knows where, if anywhere.

Yet knowing the extent of our limitation, feeling our soon-not-to-be-here-ness in our bones, is the best condition we can have for waking up to the miracle that we are here now at all. And if you think about it, that is the brilliance of the human design plan—the built-in "defect" is the very thing that can spur us to drink down the full draught as it comes to us.

How did this happen? This incredible feeling thinking sensing moving joyous painful doubting wondering life—what keeps it upright even now, right now in this unrepeatable moment that is already going, gone? No answer to that, merely the gasp of the breath as it moves in and out, and the pleasure of knowing that for now we are here and not elsewhere. Better to taste it now then, this life that we have, than to defer it to some future that may never come.

Spirit forgets the necessity of
imperfection, and that within our
very incompleteness is the
opening where love appears.
It does not understand the
essentially domestic and mortal
nature of human life.[10]

JOHN TARRANT

One of the symptoms of an
approaching nervous breakdown
is the belief that one's work
is terribly important.[1]

BERTRAND RUSSELL

FIVE

The Pleasure

of Doing

Nothing Useful

You might think there could be nothing more simple than doing nothing for no reason; doing something merely for the pleasure of it, without any thought of future profit or gain; without adding any skill or knowledge to your store, without any usefulness at all. Yet even doing nothing has now become something to do. Relaxation, the quintessential doing nothing, is something you have to "practice," and seriously, in a class for which the time slot is logged in your diary. A party is an occasion to "work the room." A weekend at the shore is an opportunity to get to know those well-connected neighbors.

A friend of mine, a magazine editor, told me recently how difficult she found it to leave her job behind. We were sitting in a restaurant in downtown Manhattan, and she was aware that she was constantly noticing the clientele, the decor, seeing if there was any angle that might work for a piece in her magazine. She longed to be able to sit down at a table without her work, to have a conversation with a friend that promised no more than the pleasure of their company. Yet her mind wouldn't let her agenda go.

We each in our own ways have an agenda. We are all lobbyists for our own cause, our own opinions, aspirations, status, or career. While there's nothing wrong with getting ahead, whatever that may mean, it can also be an enormous relief now and then to lay down our own cause and enjoy wherever we find ourselves on its own terms.

You might think that all you need do to have no agenda and do nothing in particular is to allow yourself to sit down one morning in a spontaneous sort of way in the local café without looking at your watch. And, perhaps, to ask for a china cup.

You need not leave your room.

Remain seated at your table

and listen. You need not even listen;

simply wait. You need not even wait;

just be quiet, still, and solitary.

The world will freely offer

itself to you to be unmasked.

It has no choice; it will roll

in ecstasy at your feet.[2]

FRANZ KAFKA

It's true that the cup matters. It not only affects the coffee, it also confers stability on your person. It means you are here to stay, at least in the short term. It means you are likely to be around for as much as the next half hour; that you are willing to be part of the quiet bustle and spectacle of the café *terrasse*. On a *terrasse* you are an observer and a participant at the same time, and you don't have to do anything for the privilege except to sit there. A café offers one of life's rare opportunities to happily do nothing in the company of others who are also doing nothing more useful than sipping coffee. American civic life could derive only benefit from switching to china, though I don't expect it to happen anytime soon.

Café life, without question, is one of the more enjoyable benefits of civilization. You can sit at your table for half an hour or more and watch the world go by, all for the price of a cup of coffee—or tea, if that's your preference. I know there's an irony in speaking of coffee and doing nothing in the same sentence; but the café isn't really about the coffee or tea at all. It's about the sitting there, hearing snatches of conversation, having your own thoughts, being aware of the other customers around you, watching the passersby, eavesdropping on the waiter's repartee.

Yet we are so good at being busy, we can even turn a cup of coffee into something to do. You may seem to be sitting there innocently sipping, but all the time you may be preoccupied with waiting: not just being there, but waiting for a certain amount of time to pass; waiting for your date, or for the train. Or you're busy sizing up the opposite sex. That may not seem far from doing nothing, but even so, it's not quite the same.

When you sit there and do nothing in particular at all—no waiting, no Palm Pilot, no cell phone, no agenda, nothing that will get you anywhere anytime soon—then a space can open up in your mind. Thoughts can float by without the habitual impulse to jump on their back and ride them for all they are worth. It may even happen that the taste of coffee gives way to the taste of yourself—the delicious relief of being-in-yourself.

As for waiting, there are some pleasures for which even the pleasure of the café can wait. I once spent more than the first hour of a morning in the bath of my hotel room in Paris, keeping the water hot with an occasional turn of the tap with my toe. Nothing seemed more pleasurable and fulfilling than that tubful of hot water—a tub that must have been made in the twenties, large enough for two, with claw feet and taps that stood almost six inches tall, easy for toes to play with, in a capacious bathroom of old white tiles and a large steamed-up mirror, an art deco one.

Outside there was the Louvre to visit, the Opera House to gaze at, that delicious sense of foreignness that invades the mind in any great city away from home. I am typically full of curiosity and enthusiasm for the new, but that day I felt no movement in me to get dressed and open my door. I could hear the city of cities outside my window, the drone of traffic, the tolling of a distant bell, the sporadic shouts and cries of human voices.

I knew I could accuse myself of wasting time. I knew there was the beautiful Place des Vosges to visit just around the corner, the Seine to stroll along, the wonderful district of St. Germain to meander through. But none of it seemed worth getting out of the bath for. Not that day. I must have daydreamed of this and that, the way one might also do in a comfortable armchair in front of a warm log fire; but I don't remember a single thought of any significance that passed over me during that hour or so. No, mostly I was vacant. Not in a way that was unconscious, or half-asleep, but in a way that transferred the locus of my consciousness from my mind to my body. I became a floating, wrinkly breathing white body, with arms languishing along the roll top of the tub, toes flat against the end under the old chrome taps. It is a marvel, the human body, how it can lie there happily undisturbed for as long as you care to let it, soaking in the pleasure of hot water and an empty mind, empty and alive.

An hour in a bath may not be your idea of a good time; but the point is not the bath but the rested mind that, in my case, it gave rise to. We all have our own ways. It's not what you don't do, it's the way you don't do it. The hammock did it for the poet James Wright. He wrote a whole poem about it. Lying there, he is aware of the bronze butterfly over his head, an empty house, the cowbells, a chicken hawk, and the evening darkness coming on. Then he ends with this shocking line:

I have wasted my life.[3]

As if to say that he realizes, in that hammock, that this doing nothing for no reason is the most alive and vital thing he knows; and yet he hardly ever lets himself fall into it. He echoes this thought in another poem when he writes,

I want to lie down under a tree.
This is the only duty that is not death.[4]

Wright knew the pleasure of a rested mind, though all too rarely. Without the perpetual alarm bells of what one should be doing next, of how one can gain this advantage or that, of what one should have done but didn't—without any particular purpose in mind—the cells of the body seem to settle in their rightful place and, in my case, especially when they are bathed in warm water. The mind itself becomes clear rather than clouded, as still as a lake with no wind, which is what distinguishes interior rest from the conventional sin of sloth.

It was Thomas Aquinas, the thirteenth-century thinker's man from southern Italy, who came up with the notion that sloth was a bad idea; it doesn't take a great deal of persuasion to agree with him. "Sluggishness of mind" is how he described it, and he was referring in particular to those monks who, by the time the noon bell tolled, were feeling heavy and down in both body and mind. Sloth as a kind of depression, then, a "noonday demon" that prevented them from hitting the right note in the choir stalls. Their secular equivalent today might be the couch potato, the professional slacker, or anyone with a habit of inactivity that leads to a dull and arrested mind.

There is a place in anyone's life for being bored and listless. It happens. And usually it doesn't happen for the reason we think. But the pleasure of a rested mind—rested from the necessity of always needing to be busy with something useful, to strategize, or to advance oneself in some way—is not the same as boredom. It imparts a quiet gladness, a sense of breadth and spaciousness that is made possible by dropping for a while our story of who we think we are. No matter what we are doing or not doing, true rest happens when we take a rest from ourselves.

There was a reason my long bath happened away from home. In Paris I was relieved of my sense of obligation; the self-imposed obligation to feel productive, gainfully employed, and a contributing member of society. In Paris I had no role, no part to play, no money to earn. I was invisible, and I could afford to let the world roll by without needing it to confirm my existence. I had stepped out of my familiar story for a while.

Letting the world roll by can be one of the values of drifting on a desert island in winter. Affluent New Yorkers, however, the ones who care a great deal about what others think of them, even like to vacation where they can be seen by their peers. An article in the *New York Times* recently described people from the Upper East Side turning up at a distant foreign resort, only to discover that half of their neighbors were there already. As if they didn't know they would be. As if they didn't know the resort was the latest place to be seen.

Invisible, after all, is precisely what we dread to be. Not being seen, how easy it is to feel we do not exist. And the way most of us are seen is through what we do and especially by what we produce.

For many of us, it is enough to give the impression that we are producing, whether we actually are or not. Never mind the creation of a tangible product, a piece of music, a new invention, a fired pot, a cooked dinner: no, the real currency of our time comes from producing waves, getting things moving, talking up a storm, creating an impression. The bigger our image, the more visible we are, and that is mostly what matters. The only thing more important is that we are seen to be busy.

We need people to know that the earliest we can see them is next week, and even that will be a stretch. That if we are not on the phone, we are on the Web, and whatever we are on, life is nothing but hectic, crazy right now, up to our ears in it all, our very own dust devil swirling all around us. It should all ease up in the fall, we say, though of course it never does.

We don't want it to ease up because if it did, where would we be? Who would we be? It's not pleasant to feel like a doughnut, with nothing in the middle. So we juggle balls in the air, as many as possible, so fast that we hope no one can see the empty spaces between them. Nothing, after all, can be really frightening. Feeling invisible is another way of saying we feel we are nothing, nobody, with no existence or value to speak of.

The emptiness is there because it is real; we can never locate precisely where and who we are. If we could, it would mean we were something concrete, like a liver or a lung. Wasn't it the Buddha who told us there is no individual soul to speak of (*to speak of*, meaning nothing that we can conceptualize, since who we are is beyond words). The essence of mind, I think he said, is pure space, just like the ungraspable stuff around the body and the stars. We can never point to where or who we are, because who we are in essence—not our character traits, but the source from which we live and have our being—is always ungraspable, a curl of mist on the wind, an unutterable mystery even to ourselves.

In the times I have lowered myself down there, down into the heart of the feeling of empty, a quiet, a peacefulness has come upon me that I have always been thankful for. I have sensed that the darkness, the emptiness, far from being a dead and dull thing, can be vibrant as the night sky.

Empty becomes spacious. And feeling spacious is a pleasure indeed. It allows us to feel as wide as the world.

That's all very well, you might say, but this emptiness thing can gnaw away at you like the proverbial worm, and anything is preferable to the sensation of feeling irrelevant. That's why it's better to stay busy, and that's why it's not so easy to lie back and do nothing useful.

I would agree: a morning in the bath or a hammock may not be for everyone. Yet in reality, the art of doing nothing has nothing to do with what you are doing or not doing. You can be lying in a hammock or on the beach and be furiously working schemes, daydreams, or sexual fantasies. You can be conducting an orchestra or playing tennis and be so fully in the experience that the notion of conscious will falls away and it feels like you are doing nothing at all. Then whatever you are doing seems to be doing itself somehow, whether it be making love, mowing the lawn, or taking a walk.

But we are in love with the notion of conscious will. We don't like the idea that things can happen—and especially the course of our own life—without our being there to steer the ship. Without our habitual idea of ourselves running the show, surely our lives would fall apart? Well, perhaps. And perhaps not. We all know the pleasure of those moments when self-consciousness dissolves and we are just where we are, speaking or not speaking, thinking or not thinking, busy or not busy, no big deal. In moments like these, we are following our natural inclination instead of a preconceived plan. And we can all suspect what a pleasure that might be.

So where is our precious conscious will in moments like these? The world stays on its axis, we are a lot happier than when we are trying to make life happen; yet without any extra push on our part, it's all just flowing along.

One way to experience just flowing along is to take a long ride on a train. Since my own long bath in Paris, I have discovered, as many have before me, that there is a halfway house, if you like—a pleasurable way to sustain the illusion of being useful (such an ingrained responsibility) and advancing one's cause without actually doing anything at all. This is the way of the train ride, not on a commuter train, but rather on a train journeying for several hours through unfamiliar territory.

It is a wonderful thing to ride on a train, especially through a foreign land whose railroad system is state-subsidized and therefore comfortable, with good coffee and decent food. It is literally the easiest and most satisfying way to let the world roll by. A flight is stressful—all those lines at check-in, the struggle for an aisle seat, the delays, and unless your business is paying, the cramped seat next to a large neighbor.

On the train you can allow yourself the fancy that you are indeed doing something useful. After all, there is no question that you are going somewhere; the destination is printed on your ticket. Your ticket proves that you have a point. And yet the train takes the weight off your feet. You sit back and let it do all the work for you, even as you can, with some justification, claim its work for your own; even as, in reality, you are doing absolutely nothing at all.

There might seem nothing to stop you from fretting on the train just as you might fret at home, but in fact the rolling motion serves to lull cares away and replace them with daydreaming and other useless and pleasurable mental activities that can happen on their own, and all of which can be amplified by looking out of the window. Looking out a train window does something with time: it suspends it. We ourselves are suspended between the departing and the arriving, wrapped in reverie, which unfolds in its own and not in ordinary time.

Train-reverie can give rise to thoughts and reflections of a satisfyingly nonutilitarian kind, the kind that may never have surfaced in the busyness of an ordinary day. It can return us to feelings that stem from some deeper source than the chatter of the ordinary mind, feelings that bring us closer to the marrow of who we are. It can even, if we are lucky, let us feel that emptiness we may have spent so much time running from; though on the train, where we may have nothing better to do, it can seem a positive, life-affirming experience rather than a deathly one. And it all comes just by sitting there, aimless, gazing absentmindedly (that absence is the key) out of the window at the scurrying countryside.

Then, how many great ideas, novels, plays, and poems must have been born on trains, out of that emptiness, without any deliberate intent? And we will never know, will never suspect their origins. Creative ideas often spring from just this state of doing nothing that we can be so afraid of. What seems to be utterly useless can be a source of lasting joy—which must be why John Keats wrote these lines in a letter to his friend J. H. Reynolds in 1818:

> Let us not therefore go hurrying about and collecting honey-bee like, buzzing here and there impatiently for a knowledge of what is to be arrived at: but let us open our leaves like a flower and be passive and receptive—budding patiently under

the eye of Apollo and taking hints from every noble insect that favors us with a visit.[5]

As with the train ride, so it can be with a stroll or a long walk with no particular destination, or at least with no time line to fulfill. If lying in a hammock for an afternoon without a book seems just too much of a challenge, then why not go walking and see where you end up just following the body wherever it takes you? We all take a walk from time to time, but not, I suspect, with no end in mind, no shopping, no exercise, no dog.

Walking entails more effort than sitting on a train, but it is a bodily effort, a rhythmical sway that aligns us with the gait and the pant of animals, the time of day rather than the time on the dial. Walking, not as a regimen but as an engagement with the living world, quiets the mind. This kind of walking lets us breathe more deeply and, like the train in its way, allows us a taste of doing nothing in particular, nothing more than just walking along for no reason, noticing what we may never have noticed, the top floor windows of buildings, the color of roofs.

Wordsworth, who wandered "lonely as a cloud" over hill and dale, wrote an entire autobiography in verse from the fruits of his strollings. When we walk somewhere today, it is usually to get somewhere. But Wordsworth was walking for walking's sake, rather like the Australian aboriginal, who goes on walkabout still today with the intention of laying himself open to the unknown yet fertile reaches within.

One of the many things that Wordsworth might have discovered on his walks was not only the astounding beauty of the natural world, but also the absence of any intrinsic reason for the appreciation of beauty other than the sheer pleasure of it for its own sake. The appreciation of beauty is not productive. It has no ulterior motive. It has no function above and beyond itself. It happens because it happens, in the same way a rose or a snowflake happens. Yet it is one of the greatest pleasures we can know.

When it comes to walking, some people, as Rilke reminds us, keep on walking right out of their life:

Sometimes a man stands up during supper
And walks outdoors, and keeps on walking.[6]

These people dare to drop out of an identity they may have nurtured for years; they are willing to be invisible for a period of time, without any apparent usefulness whatso-

If you can spend a perfectly
useless afternoon in a perfectly
useless manner, you have
learned how to live.[7]

LIN YUTANG

ever; and they are curious enough to see if there is anything on the other side. This is one of the most liberating,
as well as frightening, things we can do.

Veronica Goodchild is one such person. Originally
from England, she was a single mother of two children
with a flourishing psychotherapy practice on the East
Coast, midway through her Ph.D., when it began to dawn
on her that she was living from values that were not intrinsically her own. With this realization,

> the call was so strong, so insistent were the
> dreams, that within a period of two months, I had
> decided to close my therapy practice of fifteen
> years, rent my house, and return with my chil-
> dren to my roots in my native England, that I had
> left some twenty years previously in search of
> myself. . . .
>
> For almost a year, while my children attended
> the local school, and thrived on Celtic soil bathed
> in the gleam and magic aura of the grandparental
> eye, I did nothing except read novels, take exten-
> sive aromatherapy baths, surrender into dreams,
> and roam (for hours at a time) the hills surround-
> ing my parents' old farmhouse in the wild and re-
> mote west of England.

On this extended solitary walkabout, I tried to let all identities dissolve, becoming nothing and no one in particular. It was as if the personas and roles of my life receded in their definitions, in such a way that I became a human being—a woman—first, and in a sense, only that. . . . I needed to see what my life depended on when there was nothing left to hold me. In what great mystery was I held, if any at all? Could I really let go? Could I surrender, and fall into Life? Fall into the Great Below? . . .

Learning to slow down, to stand still, rather than anxiously moving on as if the world depended on my actions seems unbearable to my human form that in some ways has not yet borne itself. Neither acting nor retreating, I bear tension and paradox, in an in-between state—the place between God's and Adam's fingers in Michelangelo's depiction of Creation. . . . This ability, in this moment, to withstand, tolerate, the whole of who we are, dark and light, consciously, seems to relieve God and substantiate us.[8]

Among the many blessings she counts from that time of floating free of familiar roles, Goodchild was able to resolve her parental relations and also to meet the love of her life, with whom she eventually moved, along with her two children, to the West Coast of America.

Dropping out of our familiar identity for a while, as she did, and "into the Great Below" would be a wonderful training for later life. After all, how many men suffer heart attacks within three years of retiring? It is so easy to confuse what we do with who we are, especially perhaps for men. Many women have the same identity confusion when they are mothers.

If we are not useful, after all, what else can we be but useless? Even taking such a simple break in routine as spending a morning with your feet up, gazing out of the window, can begin to dispel that misunderstanding. A fully lived and passionate life is not only, or not even mostly, about being useful or useless, it is about being. Being what? That we shall discover only when we lay down our arms and rest awhile from being everything we think we are.

Not so long ago, a century or two, farmers would always leave one of their fields fallow. They would give that piece of their land a rest, so that it would be more fruitful in future harvests. We, however, work our fields without ceasing all through the living day. There's nothing wrong with being productive—we all know it can give a profoundly satisfying sense of achievement—but if we never let ourselves do nothing at times, our inner resources will drain away, and we shall move through our days with a pervading sense of unease. We shall not, in short, be happy.

What can anyone give you greater
than now,
Starting here, right in this room,
when you turn around?[1]

WILLIAM STAFFORD

SIX

The Pleasure

of Being

Ordinary

In my living room, near the window, is a long table with a round blue bowl on it. It must have been there for a year or more, but it's only recently that I've begun to notice that large blue bowl. Even a week ago I barely knew it was there. Now it fills me with pleasure, I don't know why. It's a thick blue bowl, a peasant of a bowl, with a fat lip running right round its rim. It holds a few grubby finger marks, a scattering of dust, a solitary lemon, and some long silver slivers of light from the window. Its blue is the rich blue of a Persian carpet. Like a peacock, that luminous blue now draws my eyes to it whenever I pass. This morning I trailed my fingers over its welcoming lip, and was surprised by the cool touch of china.

The bowl had been flashing light all along. It was only I who had to be ready to catch its glint. Not that it is especially beautiful; rather, the more I gave it the time of day, the more it glowed. They are all like that, the ordinary things that surround us every day. They come alive in the light of our attention, in our acknowledgment, even, of their existence. In your own living room catching sight of a fragment of cloth, a pattern of light on the carpet, or the curved back of a chair may open your eyes to an unexpected pleasure.

Whether you look at an object or at a person, the beauty is in the looking, not in the value or in the cheekbones. It is almost impossible to look upon any human face and feel a dislike for the person. The sheer looking reveals the individual instead of the stereotype. It replaces liking or not liking with an affinity for another living being, and that is always a pleasure.

Not only looking but giving an ear to the humdrum

events of daily life can also be strangely pleasing, including sounds that I, for one, would normally grumble about: the whirring of a pneumatic drill in the far distance, the city cicada I heard on waking this morning, the keening wind whipping at the corner of the building, the floorboards creaking in the kitchen below, the faint hiss of a kettle, and someone in the bathroom clearing their throat of phlegm.

It was an unlikely morning chorus: that, for some reason, was how I heard them all this morning, instead of as something to complain about. Unusually sensitive now to the sounds of my household, I slouched to the bathroom, turned on the shower, and heard the full throttle of the spray of water, the lapping, the rush, the gurgle of the excess down the drain, the dripping of suds down my face, the muffled rub of towel on my back, the sudden sound of my own voice talking to itself, the water sucking away—so many sounds I'll explode if I let them all in . . . voices starting into motion, the tuneless singing of a young girl, the clink of a spoon in a cup, the lapping of liquid in china, a vast orchestra of living sounds, the world announcing itself in a perpetual daily chorus of whispers and rumbles and gurgles and plaintive cries and pips and squeaks and running water blowing and calling out for no other reason than the love of being alive.

We live in a world of humdrum things and events and other ordinary people like us. Ordinary is good. Ordinary and wonderful are what life is. But you would never think so from how desperately hard most of us strive to be anything but ordinary. It's one thing to appreciate the everyday world of ordinary things that surround us, but quite another to begin to appreciate how ordinary one is oneself. According to conventional wisdom, being ordinary is definitely not cool and certainly no pleasure. It's much better secretly to feel that a special destiny is reserved for you, if only you can find the key. Being ordinary is almost a sin in a culture where the whole point is to do whatever it takes to stand out and be noticed.

I have tried to avoid the sin of being ordinary for most of my life. At the age of twenty-two, in the last semester of my degree course, I moved to a studio flat in the suburbs of Birmingham, England, to concentrate on my studies. I would work in front of a window with no curtains. Every house on the street was the same, a little patch of grass in the front with a car in the driveway. On Sunday mornings all the neighbors would be out mowing their front lawns or washing their cars.

"*That* is exactly how I am not going to spend my life," I would mutter almost every weekend. To my mind, these

Stirring the oatmeal is a humble act—
not exciting or thrilling. But it
symbolizes a relatedness that brings
love down to earth. . . . Love is
content to do many things that the
ego is bored with. Love is willing to
work with the other person's moods
and unreasonableness. Love is willing
to fix breakfast and balance the check
book. Love is willing to do these
"oatmeal" things because it is related
to a person, not a projection.[2]

ROBERT A. JOHNSON

people were corralled by conformity and cursed by a lack of imagination or aspiration. They seemed content to work all week in order to spend their free time on weekends keeping their lawns tidy and their cars clean.

Superior, I was; self-righteous, too—and, come what may, determined never to live a humdrum, ordinary life the way my father did. He was a gentle giant, a man of few words who would gaze in wonder for twenty minutes at a spider weaving its web. He was a deliveryman, worked for the same company all his life, and enjoyed nothing more than driving around the English countryside from morning till night dropping off laundry detergent and margarine to the local shops.

I could never understand why he didn't want to make more of his life, why he refused all promotion offers that could have given him a supervisor's job in the office. But he loved the independence of his driving cab, hated the prospect of office politics, and laughed off a teenager's urges to "better himself."

After college I had all the ambition my father lacked. I was sure I could do anything I wanted. I worked for a couple of years for *The Times* of London and then struck out on my own. I organized publicity events for nonprofits, I wrote articles for the press, and I did radio interviews for the BBC. Life as a freelancer, however, turned out to be tough, even if I was defining what I did on my own terms. Work, though interesting, was somewhat sporadic—I tended to follow my own interests and passions rather than willingly taking any story that was offered me, and for that I sacrificed a clear-cut career path.

As a result, by my thirties I was beginning to feel out on a limb, and that cut two ways. On the one hand, I felt little commonality with the mainstream culture and most people's priorities, goals, and concerns. That would sometimes leave me feeling isolated and misunderstood. On the other hand, that same alienation would merge into a feeling of being special, a case apart from the norm in some way.

My "specialness" protected me, gave me a way to feel worthy even in the absence of all the usual social cues by which worthiness is valued—wealth, power, and influence. And to sustain my special feeling, I was obliged to regard with a certain disdain—even if it was not consciously recognized as such at the time—those who led anonymous little lives in the cookie-cutter suburbs of London.

My specialness was, in a way, my security. It gave me a feeling of substance that perhaps others felt through their career or their wealth. I can see now that it was my way of staving off the empty feeling in my belly, the one that did not come from a lack of food. My specialness was the blanket I wrapped myself in to keep out the cold fact that, in reality, I had no idea who I was or where I was going in life.

I was different, that's all I knew, and my difference was my identity. For me, different rules applied. If I was struck by a sudden urge to wander into the Sahara Desert, I followed it. If I wanted to roam around Egypt exploring Coptic monasteries, I did that. And over and over again I would go to India. But not to drift around for the sake of it; no, being a writer and sometime photographer, I would turn almost everything I did into a project, and I am still doing the same today. If I went to India so many times, a book would have to come out of it, and it did. If I fell in love with the Sahara, then I would need somehow to tell the tale, and I did.

The more colorful and dramatic the story, the better. Yet my first experience of the Sahara was quite different from what I had expected. I was going—though I wouldn't have put it this way at the time, indeed, would have been offended by the suggestion—I was going for nothing less than to act the lead in my own movie. I wanted to know what it would be like to be way out there in the wasteland on my own for a few days. As familiar as my moods and preoccupations were to me, I wanted to get closer to myself than the habitual inner chatter; I was aware that there is a depth to human existence about which I had only the vaguest notion. Others would go to a meditation class. I went to the Sahara.

I flew from London to Algiers and from there to Tamanrasset, a small town far to the south, near the border with Niger. At the time, in 1975, Tam was a few streets of low houses, an old French caravanserai, and a fort, all constructed in adobe. On that second plane ride I sat next to a mountain of a man with a handlebar mustache who was on his way to Chad to hunt rhinoceros. I couldn't have asked for a better opening scene.

I hired a guide, and we left town just as the sun was rising. We continued until early afternoon. For hours we crossed rock-strewn plains and gullies, orange and red everywhere, until eventually we passed two slabs of rock leaning against each other to form an open-ended cave: a perfect shelter from the glare of the sun. I would stay here for three days and see what happened. My guide would then return to lead me back to town.

He led the camels back over a slight rise and disappeared. I turned to contemplate my surroundings. No

[For him] The chair is a chair, not a throne.

The boots have been worn by walking.

The sunflowers are plants, not constellations.

The postman delivers letters. The irises will die.

And from this nakedness of his,

which his contemporaries saw as naivety or

madness, came his capacity to love, suddenly at

any moment, what he saw in front of him.

Picking up pen or brush, he then strove to

achieve that love. Lover-painter affirming the

toughness of an everyday tenderness we all

dream of in our better moments and instantly

recognize when it is framed.[3]

JOHN BERGER, ON VINCENT VAN GOGH

wind, no trace of movement, no sound; everything just where it had been for centuries. Gooseflesh ran along my arms. I laid my bedroll between the rocks, heard my breathing, and felt the air pass an electricity through me. The rest of that day I sat beneath the rock in awe, with a sheer animal joy, not just at the world I had come to but at the marvel of my own living and breathing.

By the second day, though, it was all rather different. The drama and excitement of acting out a cherished dream had evaporated. There I was alone in the midst of this desolate landscape, awakened in the morning at the first glimmer of light by swarming hordes of buzzing flies. I was churning out the same ordinary thoughts, I realized (at first, with some disappointment), as I did back in London.

I found myself laughing, not in self-deprecation but in genuine amusement. I was no great ascetic or intrepid adventurer. There was nobody special waiting to be revealed beneath my humdrum exterior; no reserved destiny or Damascus experience was about to proclaim itself on the desert stage. No, beneath the tick-tock of my hopes and fears, between the thoughts of my past and future, there was nothing much to speak of at all, simply a quiet and empty space, rather like the desert itself. What had so often felt like a gap or a hole in me now felt like a source of spacious, uncomplicated aliveness.

Suddenly, there in the stark desert light I became aware of the deep insignificance of the personal story that I had imagined to be my identity. I knew that I too would pass like my own footsteps in the sand. Standing there, a speck on a vast canvas, I felt returned to proportion: true, authentic, and unashamedly small, without even a story to tell—though of course I lost no time in telling one as soon as I got back.

That desert experience was a foretaste of a long, slow change in me that has continued in fits and starts on down through my life. I continued to travel to exotic places, to seek out remote monasteries and wise men, to value the unusual and extraordinary over the quotidian. I did so because it made me feel more intensely alive. It felt like a colorful and vital way to live. And in many ways it was.

But more to the point, the color and the stories were also ways to smooth over my existential uncertainty, to help me feel I was living a "meaningful" life, whatever that is. The curiosity, the thirst for the new and for the un-known—all of it was a search for joy, for inspiration, for aliveness. But the search tended always to lead up and out—out from under the weight of daily concerns and the worries of a human being struggling to find his way in the world, out toward some clear blue foreign air free of all "lesser" preoccupations. The desert, always my favorite place, was the perfect metaphor for this rarefied clarity.

Yet right there in the Sahara I caught a glimpse of the obvious: that however much of a storm we may kick up on the outside, however exciting it may seem, it cannot ultimately disguise the fact of our inner condition, which we carry with us everywhere. Our inner condition, rather than our outer circumstance, is what truly defines us. However humble his job may have been, my father was a contented man, which is more than could be said of his son.

And beneath our content or discontent is the deeper condition we all share, whether we acknowledge it or not: we are here, we are human, a glorious nothing much to speak of, whoever we are, an essential flash in the pan whose purpose will always be in the living and not in the telling. Which doesn't make life any easier for a storyteller like me.

What this simple realization set in motion—and I am eternally grateful to the desert for this—was a growing respect for the ordinary, which is to say things as they are, whatever they are. I gradually began to doubt my value system, whereby I deemed some activities meaningful and others of little value; by which I judged the grand gesture, the bigger story, more important than the mundane and the unnoticed—though again, I would never have put it that way.

It just seemed obvious to me for many years, until Maria came into my life, and still does at times, that some activities were more "important" than others: poetry, literature, philosophical and psychological questions, and familiarity with other cultures and customs, to name just a few. There is unquestionably a place for individual taste; it's just that those who did not share my tastes didn't have much taste.

I know I am not alone with the "special" complex, and that there are different notions of what being special means. But they are united in agreeing that the ordinary, the commonplace, is not the thing to be. No one wants to be ordinary. It's the norm to want to be noticed; being special has become a cultural fetish. Designer goods have become whole industries feeding on people's need to separate themselves from the crowd.

Our celebrity culture values fame, even notoriety, above anything else. If you aren't recognizable yourself, then the next best thing is to know someone who is. Name recognition gives you more status than anything. What we want is the glow, the charisma of appearing to be "somebody," whether we have done anything worth talking about or not. Of all eras, this is surely the one where the emperor with no clothes can be king.

People flock to the latest club, the latest restaurant, in proportion to the number of celebrities who go there. In New York or L.A., the more you have to beg for a table, scream at your dinner companion to be heard, deal with a waiter who often has a more superior attitude than you do, and pay through the nose for the whole privilege, the more desirable the restaurant becomes. It is an experience I am glad to forgo.

In New York it is a pleasure for me to sit in an ordinary restaurant where I can hear what my companion is saying without having to crane my neck across the table: one like the Hudson Café on the corner of my block, with wicker chairs, gingham check tablecloths, a glass of wine for four dollars, and a perfectly decent menu prepared by a chef no one knows. To my knowledge, no one famous goes to the Hudson Café; it is not a place to be seen because it is not a scene. You can eat in peace without feeling the need to look at the other diners and without feeling that they may be looking at you. In a world where image is more valued than substance, this is a rare pleasure indeed.

Being in a restaurant full of the rich and the famous can make us feel that we have somehow "arrived"; as if simply sitting in the same restaurant as such luminaries makes us somebody of note. Back in the desert, however, the ordinary, the mundane in me, was inescapable. My surroundings were spectacular, my situation unusual. Yet it wasn't long before the rocks were hard, the sun hot, and the flies a persistent nuisance. The place gradually transformed, in a word, into nothing special at all. Within a couple of days my surroundings had become ordinary. And whatever my expectations had been, they were only a story made up by me. The desert remained the desert, impervious to the layers of meaning and no-meaning I put on it.

Even so, my value judgments and assumptions about what was important and what wasn't remained etched in my hard drive. Years later, when I came to live in America, I still had the same stories running. My son was then twenty-three, and rightly or wrongly, I felt able to follow my life to another country without abandoning him. For the previous dozen years or so my relationship had been shaped in significant degree, by the presence not only of my son (from a previous marriage) but also of my partner's daughter, even though neither of them lived with us full-time.

So among other things, my new life in America signified to me a final departure from being a family man (however imperfectly I had fulfilled the role) to being free to follow wholeheartedly the life of the wandering explorer and writer that I had always felt myself to be anyway. I would spend a year in a monastery, or perhaps start a project in Africa. And within two weeks I fell in love with a woman with three children.

I had already made plans to act out a long-cherished dream of living in or around San Francisco. Maria was living in New Jersey, and when she gave primary custody of her children to their father, she flew backward and forward between the coasts for a couple of years. I was exactly where I wanted to be, happily living and writing in our "treehouse" among the redwoods.

But gradually what had seemed inevitable to everyone but me began, like the swell of the tide, to roll in. Maria needed to live full-time near her kids, and if I wanted us to stay together, I would have to sacrifice my warm California idyll for the pleasure of her company in New Jersey.

I was willing to leave the treehouse for the East Coast

but not yet ready to take on New Jersey. I had never set foot there (why would I?), but in my mind it was not so different from my window view in my last year in college, suburban and conventional, conservative values, family values—whatever that means—being foremost. Forcing myself to accept that would be pushing myself too far. So at first we tried a compromise and moved to upstate New York, to artsy Woodstock, where at least I knew a few people and where we thought, after California, we would be in a community of like-minded people.

And we were. But it is cold in Woodstock, very cold, and a long way from anywhere. I had not emigrated all the way from England to set up home in four months of snow. It was a three-hour ride to Maria's kids, and a long way in the mind from New York. We lasted eighteen months and then did what we perhaps should have done to begin with—except I hadn't been ready. We found a miniature studio in Manhattan and a little house in Jersey just two blocks from the children's school.

It's all still quite new, and just as in the desert, feelings and perceptions can undoubtedly change with the time of day. But speaking for now, I love this little house in suburbia, with just enough space to cater to everyone's needs. The children run in and out and come home for lunch in the middle of school. And I am enjoying them. I enjoy playing Scrabble and cards with them and helping with homework. I feel much less than I used to that my attention is being diverted from more important things, and I rarely resent them for it; though it still happens— the noise level reaches a certain pitch, my mind runs the same thought, reads the same sentence a dozen times over, and I no longer know where I am. Just like any parent, I imagine.

Earlier in my life I would have seen this to be a terrible distraction from more important concerns. I was intense. I still am, I suppose, but now at least it's no longer a matter of life and death. All life will not cease if I do not get my thought down on a page, if I am hopelessly dispersed and fragmented for an hour or even a day. The world can, I know now, carry on wonderfully without me. And it won't be down on me for going unconscious for a while, for not doing my share.

In fact, this *is* doing my share. At this point my given share includes noisy children in New Jersey and losing it at times. And I can happily declare that I give no thought to what living in this way might say about me. After all, what does it say about me? That I'm an ordinary guy doing ordinary things? Yes, and that too is a pleasure.

It is a pleasure to take a scary ride at the fairground with a nine-year-old girl and to go for hot chocolate afterward. It's a pleasure to have a cat, a black one named Wizard. I have not had a pet since I myself was nine years old. I truly enjoy the way he gives himself so readily to the children's attentions, the way he lets them hold him like a baby, the way he crooks his head when I stroke his neck.

It sounds almost silly, so obvious and run of the mill. "So what's new?" you might say. Millions of people all over the country know these kinds of pleasures on a daily basis and could have told me what I was missing out on a long time ago. But I wouldn't have heard them until now. It is new for me, and it has happened almost without my being aware of the change: the change, primarily, in how I regard myself.

I can't say why or how, but my edges have softened. Some of my friends are skeptical of the life I have taken on and don't expect it to last all that long. Not many men, they say, would take on a relationship with three children, especially not at the age of sixty. And especially not you. Maybe so. Yet this feels as right as anything ever has, even if it's not always easy. It has taken me a long time to get here, wherever here is, and anyway it is nothing, nothing special, no big deal.

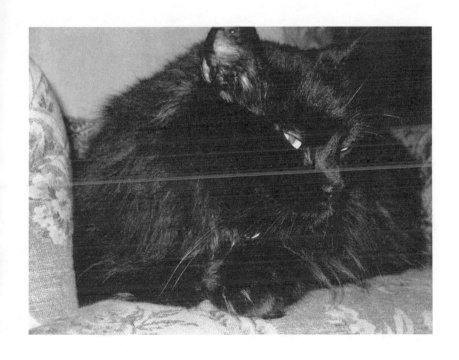

I didn't consciously do anything; it wasn't any kind of exercise in self-improvement or "doing the right thing"; it's just that here is where I am. I allowed myself to follow the thread of my life, and it brought me to a place where stroking the cat is not more but also not less of a pleasure than watching a lion lie in wait for a zebra. It led me to sharing my life with a woman from the Midwest who loves doughnuts, and who also happens to be one of the most interesting and alive people I have ever met.

And of course, an "ordinary" day is no better than a "special" one. Mr. Regular Guy is no more an acceptable posture than Mr. Special. A posture is a posture, whatever it is. And however ordinary or remarkable a day may be, we probably won't be awake or present enough to catch all of it anyway.

Yet let us be thankful for small mercies, for those moments of beauty and recollection, moments of aliveness, that we do manage to salvage from the deluge of our days. Like the sounds from the bathroom that greeted me this morning. Because even if it's true that so much of my life slips past me as in a dream, that's okay; that's why the moments we do rescue are so precious. Like all rare things, they are both ordinary and marvelous, just as we are.

At twenty, we worry about what others think of us; at forty, we don't care what they think of us; at sixty, we discover they haven't been thinking about us at all.

BOB HOPE,
QUOTED IN THE LONDON *DAILY MAIL*

I had rather be on my farm than be emperor of the world.

GEORGE WASHINGTON

SEVEN

The Pleasure

of Coming Home

The famous scene by Michelangelo in the Sistine Chapel, the one where Adam is stretching out his arm toward the hand of God, and there's just a millimeter of distance between them, is probably famous in part because of the chord that little gap strikes in people everywhere. We probably all feel like this at one time or another, everything seeming just within our reach, well almost, only a millimeter away. That millimeter of distance can feel like a mile at times. It can set us off running all over the earth in search of some rainbow's end.

I felt it once when I was out one day walking where I always used to walk, down across the Seven Acres Field toward Bailey's Wood, crossing the stream on the way. Down by the hazelnut trees, bare then in winter, I stopped as I always stopped to gaze at the green band of hills surrounding me like arms and the lone oak tree that used to fill up with sunlight. I looked, and to my surprise and pain, it all seemed suddenly different that day. I could see the beauty of it all, but for the first time as an outsider. I was not immersed in it as I usually was. That day the soft glow of the landscape seemed unable to penetrate my skin. For the first time I felt too old for the valley. It was my birthday. I was twelve, and I felt as if I were standing on the edge of two worlds, which I was. I turned and went back home, not being able to do what I always did, not quite knowing what to do instead. Life, coming of age, had kicked me out of the nest, and so the idea of the perfect—a place or condition I knew but was now separate from—sprang alive in me. I have rarely stopped dreaming since.

When you have spent much of your life wanting to be

other than where you are, or wanting conditions to be somehow different from what they are, it comes as a relief to begin to know the pleasure of feeling at home, both in yourself and in the world. My own adventure, like that of many others, has been that of the prodigal son; and like him, my wanderings have, over a lifetime, led me back to home ground.

This is what Henry Miller means when he says, in *The Colossus of Maroussi,*

The wise man has no need to journey forth; it is the fool who seeks the pot of gold at the rainbow's end. But the two are fated to meet and unite. They meet at the heart of the world, which is the beginning and the end of the path.[1]

"Straying maps the path," the poet Rumi said. If we follow its thread, our sense of lack, our seeking and longing, may in the fullness of time lead us back to ourselves, to an eventual familiarity with the feeling of being at home in our own skin. It is a pleasure, finally to begin to come home to the body, our earthly home; to be fully embodied in this physical existence without wishing we were in the more rarefied realm of the angels; without, in fact, wishing we were anywhere but where we are. That's when we fall into ourselves, and it is a relief indeed.

Sometimes life even falls into place of its own accord. All it need take is a good landscape to feel at home in the world. The work of many American poets and writers—Gary Snyder on the West Coast, Mary Oliver on the East, Terry Tempest Williams in Utah, Barry Lopez in Oregon—is rooted in a local environment, one that sustains and supports them wherever they go.

The land of these writers is big and rugged, colorful and wild. My own setting could not be more different. I grew up in St. Catherine's Valley, a steep cleft in a Cotswold ridge on the edge of Bath, in England. Along the valley lay St. Catherine's Court, with its tiny whitewashed church. Originally, it had been a retreat house for the monks of the abbey in medieval Bath. When I was growing up, an old lady owned it. She let me ramble freely over the sprawling grounds, and I would spend hours absorbed in a fairy-tale world of ancient fishponds, tall grasses, and the drunken tombstones in the tiny churchyard.

St. Catherine's Court and chapel were as big as the world for me then, and they were my refuge for years: a refuge from the small village where I grew up, with its bickering, sullen neighbors, and where my family, who moved there from London when I was seven, were always treated as outsiders. Since I lacked much sense of home in the wider community, the land and its ancient buildings gave me my first sense of belonging.

In my later teens my attention shifted to the chapel itself, and I would spend many an afternoon there entombed in the silence. I would wonder at the monks who had built this stone vault: what they were looking for, why they had forsaken the life of ordinary men to live in this lonely valley far from the town. I would wonder at the peace that seemed to descend on me whenever I stayed in that place alone: what it was, where it came from, and why it seemed to fade away when I returned to the everyday world beyond the gates.

Then one day my sense of home grew suddenly larger. I had decided to cycle some twenty miles beyond the valley to the east, to the stone circle of Avebury. Avebury filled me with awe. There, for the first time, I knew beyond doubt that life was not merely what everyone seemed to take for granted. Here, in the midst of our local and familial preoccupations, was this staggering testament to another world, a circle of stones big enough to contain a village, great fingers pointing to the sky for almost five thousand years.

For now she need not think about
anybody. She could be herself, by herself.
And that was what now she often felt
the need of—to think; well not even to
think. To be silent; to be alone. All the
being and the doing, expansive,
glittering, vocal, evaporated; and one
shrunk, with a sense of solemnity,
to being oneself; a wedge-shaped core
of darkness, something invisible to
others. . . . Not as oneself did one find
rest ever, in her experience, but as a
wedge of darkness. Losing personality,
losing the fret, the hurry, the stir; and
there rose to her lips always some
exclamation of triumph over life when
things came together in this peace,
this rest, this eternity.[2]

VIRGINIA WOOLF

I marveled at the people who had dreamed up this circle with a processional walkway some two miles long leading to a hill just over the horizon. The whole area was alive with the presence of a mysterious culture we knew almost nothing about. On the edge of Avebury itself was Silbury Hill, one of the greatest unsolved archaeological mysteries of Europe: a huge earth pyramid that must have taken thousands of men years to erect, and still no one knows for what purpose.

That day, on my first visit to Avebury, I sat on top of Silbury Hill, a crescent moon rising, the chalk land fading into mist along the edge of the horizon, and I felt my place in the wide circle of the human family. I felt the living presence of all those who had been in that land before me, and those who were still to come; and I knew that, through time and also through space, we were of one kind. Those feelings live on in me still, though I forget them and remember them again, over and over.

Whoever is quite without their landscape?

said W. H. Auden in his poem "Detective Story."[3] I know what he means. Our early environment, especially, forms a landscape in the imagination that accompanies us wherever

we go. That inner landscape can serve as a home, a consolation; it can even give rise to great works of art or literature. But it serves best when it brings us back to where we
belong, to the sense of being at home in our own skin.

Not being embodied is a real pain in the neck. We
move in little jerks, all angularity and awkwardness. We
tense, we strain, we push, we pull, we never move easy.
We drop dishes, as I did this morning. Or we float about
with our head in some cloud of our own making, all waft-
ing dreams and half-thoughts and no feet on the ground.
But being in the body—willingly and gratefully acknowl-
edging that this is who we are and where we belong—
naturally gives rise to the pleasure of presence, and you
always know when you are in the vicinity of someone like
that.

You know because you yourself start to feel more at
ease, more present than you were the moment before.
Presence is catching, and it's a good thing to catch.
Someone with presence imparts a feeling of substance, a
confidence that is reassuring, at home with itself. That's a
nourishing feeling for those in the vicinity, whereas
charisma can feed off people. Presence extends energy
outward, but charisma draws energy toward itself from
others.

When we are present, we have a natural grace, however large or small we may be, just as the elephant has grace in its way and the gazelle in another. All animals have presence, and from them we can assume that this is the usual property of a body whose occupant is home.

Having presence is not so easy, of course, when you feel you have to keep up a good face and put on a good front, like the character in D. H. Lawrence's novel *The Princess*:

> He was always charming, courteous, perfectly gracious, in that hushed, musical voice of his. But absent. When all came to all, he just wasn't there.[4]

It's painful trying to keep up appearances; it's not easy to be at home with yourself when most of your attention is consumed in trying to make a good impression; when you are more concerned with what others think about you than what you think yourself.

Perhaps presence is a quality that comes with age. Usually it has to be worked for, since most of us have become divided selves in one form or another on our way through life.

D. H. Winnicott, the English psychologist, said that

The aim of psychoanalysis, still unfulfilled and still only half-conscious, is to return our souls to our bodies, to return ourselves to ourselves, and thus to overcome the state of self-alienation.[5]

Presence doesn't come free—especially if you opt for the psychoanalysis route—but it's not money that's needed so much as intention. Sometimes, when we notice we have been absent for a while, all it takes is the decision to sit down in our favorite chair in our own company, to go for a walk on our own, or to watch the sunset and at the same time to be aware of the rise and fall of our own breath in the belly. Then we can begin to feel sufficient to ourselves and remember how much of a pleasure even the mere act of breathing can be.

I have never known anyone speak about the pleasure of breathing with such obvious delight as Thich Nhat Hanh. He is the Buddhist monk who organized the care of the dying and wounded in Saigon during the Vietnam War. His advice to the thousands of monks and lay helpers under his guidance was to pick up the broken bodies while continuing to breathe deeply from the belly.

The breath became their anchor in the extreme circumstances. It helped keep them from being swept away

Solitude, in the sense of being

often alone, is essential

to any depth of meditation or

of character: and solitude in the

presence of natural beauty

and grandeur, is the cradle

of thoughts and aspirations which

are not only good for the

individual, but which society

could ill do without.[6]

JOHN STUART MILL

by their own or others' emotional distress. But the breath served another function: the same air passes in and out of everyone's lungs, so breathing is our most direct connection to everything else that lives and breathes. In asking his monks to breathe with attention, he was asking them to become sensitive to the one current that passes through victim, persecutor, and helper and that unites them all in the ceaseless round of life and death. Attending to their breath, the monks were practicing compassion.

Surely the old monk was stretching a point, I thought, when I heard him tell the story, then go on to sing the praises of the pleasure of breathing. After all, I have been breathing for a long time now without being aware of any particular pleasure—without, in fact, being aware of it at all. So I let my attention follow my breath down into the depths of my belly and up again. And sure enough, within a few moments, I became aware of the sheer pleasure of being alive. And it struck me that I couldn't think of any greater or more freely available pleasure than that.

By being aware of the passage of breath—not doing anything with it or trying to change it, just noticing it—I realize that we are all literally feeding on air, joined in one great circle of breath that joins not only the living but also the dead. Because the air that passed through the lungs of the deceased is still giving life to our own life now.

Sitting there allowing the breath to pass through us, we may become aware that it isn't we who are breathing so much as life that is breathing us. There is no effort involved in breathing; the rising and falling happens of its own accord; and it can bring a quiet joy, the joy of life streaming through us and all things, imparting its essence with a generosity impervious to rank or station. Breathing is pleasure on tap for free.

It wasn't long before the breathing, or my awareness of it, gathered me into a nourishing silence, and I remembered what a help silence can be in coming home to ourselves. I can't imagine being able to keep my mind on my breath in a situation like war-torn Saigon, but I know that sitting somewhere comfortable in silence allows my attention more easily to fall back into the body, allows me to feel my heartbeat, notice the easing tensions in my limbs, and free myself from the grip of habitual thinking.

But what distinguishes silence and solitude from loneliness and boredom? Being there, not as some restless interior monologue, but as a breathing, earthy aliveness. One that is moved, stirred by life; one that feels part of the larger stream of existence. When we are an embodied presence, we are grounded in the present. Which doesn't mean we can't fly—it simply means that we don't lose touch with our ground, which is our body and also the earth. *Human, humor, humble, humus*—all these words have the same roots, which lead back to the earth and the soil.

One of the true pleasures of my previous relationship was the silence we used to share every morning, an intentional silence during which we sat together for half an hour. That silence was a genuine intimacy, deeper than words can say: a union of lives for a span of time, a communion, not only with each other but with the greater life that breathed life into us both.

This in itself was a form of homecoming. And it's true that as one falls present to oneself, it is more natural to be present with others. At home in your own skin, it is more likely you will feel at home, not only with your intimate others, but also in the world.

This intimacy is the real heart of a physical home. Whatever it is that is precious to us—in my case, the cat, the faded rose armchair, and the cherished Persian rug— combines to evoke a presence that is uniquely our own. And not only possessions but colors, too. Our New Jersey house is now all bright yellows and orange with the kitchen in green. It's too much for some but just right for us. Every time I come in the front door, I feel welcomed by the glow.

A friend in New York, on the other hand, has always

loved the cool clarity of white. His furniture, the walls, even the floor is a shade of white, and he takes as much pleasure as we do in returning home. It's not the color scheme, it's the match with oneself that provides the homecoming.

Surely we owe it to ourselves to make a home, whether on our own or with another, that is a reflection of the best of who we are. This is home as sanctuary: a reflection less of our budget than of our intimacy with ourselves. Hayden Carruth finds a poem in the ecstasy he feels

as I sit in my broken
chair that cats have shredded.[7]

Carruth was on his own that night, enjoying the pleasure of his own company. Solitude is one of our most underrated pleasures, perhaps because of its (mistaken) association with loneliness. The difference lies in our presence or absence: it's absence that makes for alone and lonely. Presence—being at home—doesn't depend on company.

It's one thing to enjoy a sunset on your own, or a stroll in the woods; another to take pleasure, for example, in dining alone. A meal is usually a communal affair in

Every journey has a secret destination
of which the traveler is unaware.

MARTIN BUBER

which, ideally at least, the courses are leavened with good conversation. How easy it can be, on our own, to settle for a few scraps from the fridge rather than a meal carefully prepared by our own hand. How much more satisfying it is when we make the effort to set our place at the table, light a candle, even, and make dinner for ourselves on the stove.

Housden sits down with Housden, serves himself a butternut soup tinged with ginger, followed by salmon in dill sauce and asparagus, served on a thick dinner plate from Mexico, hand-painted with purple grapes and yellow flowers, all accompanied by a good Sauvignon Blanc. A few moments of savoring my empty plate and the yellow light in the room, another glass of that excellent Sauvignon, then comes a mango, green skin turned to yellow and orange at either end, all sweetness and a hint of asperity, and all of it unfolding in the pleasure of my own company.

Another solitary pleasure I have known is to sit at the back of a chapel on an old oak pew below a white dove descending in a narrow window of stained glass. I returned recently to the chapel of St. Catherine's Court after an absence of many years. The little building was full of shadow; it was like sitting in a whitewashed cave. I sat in the gloom and the silence and let my eyes fall closed. How long I sat there I do not know, but it was long enough to become unusually still.

Then suddenly, out of nowhere, a voice seemed to ring through the quiet of my body: *Just rest*, it said. *Just rest.* It wasn't a thought, it was a sound, as clear and loud as day. I had thought I was already at rest, but as I heard these words I was instantly aware of the subtle effort I had been making all along to be aware of the silence I was in. Even that small ripple of an effort was a residual holding back from being where I was completely. I let the silence take me then, hold me; and in that moment I became the silence. I was the silence.

For those few precious moments—or who knows, perhaps it was an hour or more—time hung suspended, and I became who I was, who we all are, the spacious ground that surrounds and suffuses all things. All my strivings, all my questionings, all my aspirations and disappointments, everything had fallen away to reveal this. I had come home, and I knew then that it was good.

From joy springs all creation.

By joy it is sustained,

Toward joy it proceeds,

And to joy it returns.

MUNDAKA UPANISHAD

What's God

Got to

Do with It?

In the beginning was the big bang. Oh, what a glorious, orgasmic, explosive beginning that was! The earth and all that lives and breathes on it is the progeny of that extended delight. We were born, not only from pain, but also from pleasure. We carry the seeds of that original delight in our genetic memory. We are a brief flare of life blazing out of the darkness before falling back into the great emptiness from which we have come. "Bliss emptiness" is what the Tibetans call our original nature, and that sounds good enough to me.

But if we all burst out of nothing and return to nowhere, then what does a mystical poet like Rumi mean with a line like this?

I don't know, only you do, what makes my heart sing.

We don't know who the "you" is he speaks to here; nor do we know what makes our own heart sing. Here we are, with the pleasure of an impossible question again. Impossible, that is, if we have more faith than belief, since faith is a gesture of arms open wide, an invitation to revelation, which can come only if we don't already have a ready answer.

Since we don't know, we can pretend. We can make up a story. And this is my story. The "you" and the singing in the human heart are one and the same. Our song is an echo of the original delight that rippled into the universe when it all began. Our happiness, our value as a person, are all in our song, and when we sing it, however deep or high the notes may be, then if there's a God, she becomes a living god. Then the world takes deep pleasure in our presence among the living, and we shall know that whatever the pain and the joy of it, the singing was worth it.

notes

INTRODUCTION

1. Theodore Roethke, "Moss-Gathering," *Straw for the Fire: From the Notebooks of Theodore Roethke 1943–63* (New York: Doubleday, 1972).

ORIGINAL PLEASURE

1. Helen Keller, *The Open Door* (New York: Doubleday, 1957).

2. Walt Whitman, "Song of Myself," *Leaves of Grass* (Philadelphia: David McKay, 1891).

ONE
THE PLEASURE OF ALL FIVE SENSES

1. Nikos Kazantzakis, *Zorba the Greek* (New York: Simon & Schuster, 1901).

2. D. H. Lawrence, "The Painted Tombs of Tarquinia," *D. H. Lawrence and Italy: Twilight in Italy, Sea and Sardinia, Etruscan Places* (New York: Penguin, 1997).

3. Salman Rushdie, *Imaginary Homelands: Essays and Criticism 1981–1991* (New York: Penguin/Granta, 1991).

4. John Tarrant, *The Light Inside the Dark: Zen, Soul, and the Spiritual Life* (New York: HarperCollins, 1998).

5. D. H. Lawrence, *Women in Love* (New York: Penguin Books, 1995).

TWO

THE PLEASURE OF BEING FOOLISH

1. Wes Nisker, "Fool's Paradise," *Inquiring Mind* (Spring 2005).

2. Kahlil Gibran, *The Prophet* (New York: Alfred A. Knopf, 1923).

3. William Blake, *The Marriage of Heaven and Hell* (London, 1790–1793).

THREE

THE PLEASURE OF NOT KNOWING

1. D. H. Lawrence, "The Painted Tombs of Tarquinia," *D. H. Lawrence and Italy: Twilight in Italy, Sea and Sardinia, Etruscan Places* (New York: Penguin, 1997).

2. Mary Oliver, "A Summer Day," *New and Selected Poems,* (Boston: Beacon Press, 1992).

3. Toinette Lippe, *Caught in the Act: Reflections on Being, Knowing, and Doing* (New York: Jeremy P. Tarcher, 2004).

4. Suzuki Roshi, quoted in David Chadwick, *Crooked Cucumber: The Life and Zen Teaching of Shunryu Suzuki* (New York: Broadway Books, 1999).

5. Heinz Pagels, *Perfect Symmetry: The Search for the Beginning of Time* (New York: Simon & Schuster, 1985).

FOUR

THE PLEASURE OF NOT BEING PERFECT

1. Celeste Biever, "Microchip Imperfections Could Cut Cloning," *New Scientist,* October 4, 2004.

2. Michel de Montaigne, "That the Taste of Good and Evil Depends on the Opinion We Have of Them," *Selected Essays* (multiple editions).

3. Walt Whitman, "Crossing Brooklyn Ferry," *Leaves of Grass* (Philadelphia: David McKay, 1891).

4. T. S. Eliot, "East Coker," *The Four Quartets* (New York: Harcourt, 1943).

5. Joel Garreau, *Radical Evolution: The Promise and Peril of Enhancing Our Minds, Our Bodies—and What It Means to Be Human* (New York: Doubleday, 2005).

6. Leonard Cohen, "Anthem," *The Future* (Sony, 1992).

7. Rumi, "Love Dogs," trans. Coleman Barks with John Moyne, in *The Essential Rumi* (San Francisco: HarperSanFrancisco, 1995).

8. Robert Bly, "Listening to the Köln Concert," *Loving a Woman in Two Worlds* (New York: Doubleday, 1985).

9. Geoff Dyer, *Yoga for People Who Can't Be Bothered to Do It* (New York: Pantheon, 2003).

10. John Tarrant, *The Light Inside the Dark: Zen, Soul, and the Spiritual Life* (New York: HarperCollins, 1998).

FIVE

THE PLEASURE OF DOING NOTHING USEFUL

1. Bertrand Russell, *The Conquest of Happiness* (New York: Liveright Publishing, 1996).

2. Franz Kafka, *The Great Wall of China and Other Stories* (Harmondsworth, Engl.: Penguin, 1991).

3. James Wright, "Lying in a Hammock at William Duffy's Farm in Pine Island, Minnesota," *Collected Poems* (Middletown, Conn.: Wesleyan University Press, 1971).

4. James Wright, "A Prayer to Escape the Marketplace," ibid.

5. John Keats, *John Keats: Poems and Selected Letters* (multiple editions).

6. Rainer Maria Rilke, "Sometimes a Man Stands Up," in *Selected Poems of Rainer Maria Rilke*, trans. Robert Bly (New York: Harper & Row, 1981).

7. Lin Yutang, *The Importance of Living* (New York: Morrow, 1996).

8. Veronica Goodchild, *Eros and Chaos: The Sacred Mysteries and Dark Shadows of Love* (Berwick, Me.: Nicolas-Hays, Inc., 2001).

SIX

THE PLEASURE OF BEING ORDINARY

1. William Stafford, "You Reading This, Be Ready," *The Way It Is* (St. Paul, Minn.: Graywolf Press, 1999).

2. Robert A. Johnson, *We: Understanding the Psychology of Romantic Love* (San Francisco: HarperCollins, 1983).

3. John Berger, *The Shape of a Pocket* (New York: Pantheon, 2001).

SEVEN

THE PLEASURE OF COMING HOME

1. Henry Miller, *The Colossus of Maroussi* (New York: New Directions, 1975).

2. Virginia Woolf, *To the Lighthouse* (multiple editions).

3. W. H. Auden "Detective Story," *Collected Poems* (New York: Vintage Books, 1991).

4. D. H. Lawrence, *The Princess and Other Stories* (New York: Penguin, 1971).

5. D. W. Winnicott, *Home Is Where We Start From: Essays by a Psychoanalyst* (New York: W. W. Norton, 1986).

6. John Stuart Mill, *Principles of Political Economy* (multiple editions).

7. Hayden Carruth, "Ecstasy," in *Scrambled Eggs & Whiskey: Poems 1991–1995* (Port Townsend, Wa.: Copper Canyon Press, 1996).

credits

Grateful acknowledgment is made to the following for permission to use their photographs:

Jo Edkins: Hampton Court maze, www.gwydir.demon.co.uk/jo/maze/branch.htm.

Rowan Gabrielle: Maria Housden.

Emiliano Marrucchi Locatelli: lunch outside at Pieve di Caminino, Tuscany, www.caminino.com.

Therese Stonehart: *The Cracked Pot*, acrylic on stone, painted by Therese Stonehart, Stonehart Art on Stone, Paulden, AZ.

Courtesy of the author: the hammock, Wizard the cat, and the door.

Grateful acknowledgment is made to the following for permission to reprint their excerpts:

Doubleday: "Listening to the Köln Concert" from *Loving a Woman in Two Worlds* by Robert Bly. Copyright © 1985 by Robert Bly. Reprinted by permission of Doubleday, a division of Random House, Inc.

Nicolas-Hays, Inc.: *Eros and Chaos: The Sacred Mysteries and Dark Shadows of Love* by Veronica Goodchild. Copyright © 2001 by Veronica Goodchild. Reprinted by permission of Nicolas-Hays, Inc.

acknowledgments

*M*y gratitude first to all those authors whose words I have borrowed to enhance the work. To Joy Harris, a true support and ally as my agent; to my wonderful editor, Toinette Lippe, who, as ever, manages to contribute both enthusiasm and an eagle eye to my overall work; and finally, to my publisher, Shaye Areheart, whose continued support and discerning intelligence would be a gift for any author.

about the author

Roger Housden, a native of Bath, England, emigrated to the United States in 1998. He now lives in New York City and Fair Haven, New Jersey, with his wife, Maria. His books explore the existential and spiritual issues of our time. His most recent works include *How Rembrandt Reveals Your Beautiful, Imperfect Self: Life Lessons from the Master; Ten Poems to Last a Lifetime; Ten Poems to Set You Free; Risking Everything: 110 Poems of Love and Revelation; Ten Poems to Open Your Heart; Chasing Rumi: A Fable About Finding the Heart's True Desire;* and *Ten Poems to Change Your Life.*